D0324275

GLASSES

· AND ·

CONTACT

LENSES

ALSO BY
DR. ALVIN AND VIRGINIA B.
SILVERSTEIN

Alcoholism

Allergies

Cancer: Can It Be Stopped?

Epilepsy

Headaches: All About Them

Heartbeats: Your Body, Your Heart

Heart Disease: America's #1 Killer

Runaway Sugar: All About Diabetes

Sleep and Dreams

So You're Getting Braces: A Guide to Orthodontics

The Sugar Disease: Diabetes

GLASSES

Your Guide to Eyes,

· AND ·

Eyewear, & Eye Care

CONTACT

Dr. Alvin & Virginia B. Silverstein

LENSES

J. B. LIPPINCOTT  NEW YORK

For Leo and Elizabeth Babeu

Glasses and Contact Lenses: Your Guide to Eyes, Eyewear, and Eye Care

Copyright © 1989 by Alvin and Virginia B. Silverstein
Printed in the U.S.A. All rights reserved.
Typography by Carol Barr
1   2   3   4   5   6   7   8   9   10
First Edition

Library of Congress Cataloging-in-Publication Data
Silverstein, Alvin.
    Glasses and contact lenses.

    Bibliography: p.
    Includes index.
    Summary: Explains the structure of the eye, how vision works, and how glasses
and contact lenses correct vision problems. Also discusses exercises to improve
vision and types of conditions that require corrective surgery.
    1. Eyeglasses—Juvenile literature.   2. Contact lenses—Juvenile literature.
3. Vision—Juvenile literature.   4. Eye—Care and hygiene—Juvenile literature.
[1. Eyeglasses.   2. Contact lenses.   3. Vision.   4. Eye—Care and hygiene.]   I.
Silverstein, Virginia B.   II. Title.
RE976.S55   1989   617.7'522   88-13026
ISBN 0-397-32184-8
ISBN 0-397-32185-6 (lib. bdg.)

ILLUSTRATION
CREDITS

Illustrations on pages 15, 16, 18, 21, 25, 27, 34, 40, 44, 115, by Joel Katz/ Melissa Turk and The Artist Network
Other credits: Better Vision Institute, Inc., pages 4, 46, 56, 73, 87, 96, 106, 126
W. Poulet, *Atlas on the History of Spectacles*, 3 vols., Bonn—Bad Godesburg, Verlag J.P. Wayenborgh (1978–1980), pages 5, 6, 10, 52, 59
Bausch & Lomb, pages 12, 29, 61, 90
Reprinted with permission of the author, Alvin Silverstein, from *Human Anatomy and Physiology*, John Wiley and Sons, Inc. (1980), pages 30, 33, 37
Dr. Norman Bailey, O.D., and Bich Nguyen, with the University of Houston College of Optometry, pages 67, 70, 73, 75
Richmond Products, page 69
Reprinted with permission of the American Academy of Opthalmology, page 72
Courtesy Logo Paris, Inc., Novato, California, page 80
Courtesy American Optometric Association, pages 94, 109
Illustrations provided by the Optometric Extension Program Foundation, a nonprofit foundation committed to education and research in behavioral optometric care. For more information contact the OEP Foundation at 2912 S. Daimler, Santa Ana, CA 92705-5811, or (714) 250-8070, page 125

ACKNOWLEDGMENTS

The authors would like to thank Dr. Judith E. Gurland for her careful reading of the manuscript and her many helpful and insightful comments and suggestions. Thanks also to Michael H. Senft of the Better Vision Institute and all the others who so generously supplied illustrations and information. And special thanks to our editor, Christiane Deschamps, for her perceptive insights and encouragement.

CONTENTS

SO YOU NEED GLASSES

PERHAPS you've been having trouble seeing the blackboard or the television screen clearly. Or the print looks blurry when you try to read a book. Maybe people have been noticing that you tend to rub your eyes or squint a lot. Or perhaps you thought everything was fine, but you couldn't read all the letters on the 20/20 line of the eye chart in a routine physical exam. And now the doctor says you need glasses.

Or perhaps you're just curious. Maybe a friend recently started wearing glasses, and you're wondering what is wrong and how the glasses can help. Perhaps your mother just got a prescription for reading glasses, after a few years of asking you to thread needles for her and using a magnifying glass to look up numbers in the phone book.

Maybe you're already wearing glasses, but you still have some unanswered questions. Just what is wrong with your eyes? How can glasses help you to see better? Will you have to wear glasses all your life? Could you—and should you—switch to contact lenses?

If you wear glasses (or need to), you have plenty of company. Studies show that about 50 percent of Americans wear prescription eyewear, and that does not include the many people who buy over-the-counter eyeglasses from drugstores or mail-order catalogs. One federal study estimated that 60 percent of the work force needs corrective lenses. Eyeglass wearers range from very young children to the very old. All together, people in the United States spend about eight billion dollars on eye care and eyewear each year!

The working parts of a pair of glasses are its lenses. A *lens* is a transparent object that changes the path of light rays, focusing them to form an image. Each of your eyes has a lens. Normally the natural lenses of the eyes can form clear images of objects around us, whether they are close or very distant. But sometimes there are imperfections in the lenses, in the eye muscles that work with them, or in the shape of the eyeballs. Then the images that we see may be blurry or distorted.

Corrective lenses made of glass or plastic can be used to compensate for such imperfections, yielding a clear, sharp image. *Eyeglasses* (sometimes called spectacles) consist of such lenses, together with a framework to hold them in place in front of the eyes. *Contact lenses* are placed directly in contact with the surface of the eyes.

Eyewear Through the Ages

We tend to take eyeglasses for granted today. When they were first invented, though, they seemed like a miracle—or black magic. A piece of clear glass or crystal, placed in front of the eye, could suddenly make things look larger and clearer.

No one is quite sure who invented eyeglasses, but it probably happened in the thirteenth century. The first written mention of eyeglasses dates back to 1268, when an early English scientist, Roger Bacon, wrote in his *Opus Majus* that people with weak eyes could read even small print with the aid of "crystal or glass or other transparent substance, if it be shaped like the lesser segment of a sphere, with the convex side towards the eye." Bacon was a Franciscan friar, and his scientific experiments and daring ideas were regarded with suspicion and fear by many of his contemporaries. He was actually sent to prison twice, on charges of dabbling in black magic. During his first time in prison, though, he sent Pope Clement IV a gift of magnifying lenses for reading.

It was probably a friend of Bacon's, Heinrich Goethals, who carried the idea of eyeglasses to Italy. In 1285, on a journey to Rome, Goethals met Alessandro

Eyewear through the ages.

This illustration from a volume of music, Canzoni Nove *(ca. 1510), shows a pince-nez style of eyeglasses.*

della Spina, a monk in Pisa who had a gift for making copies of devices based on sight or a mere description. Della Spina began making eyeglasses, which, according to the records of his monastery, he "distributed with a cheerful and benevolent heart."

Another Italian is also linked with the invention of eyeglasses. During the same trip, Goethals visited the city of Florence, where he met Salvino d'Armato. Whether d'Armato later claimed to have invented eyeglasses or the claim was made for him by enthusiastic customers is not known. In any case, his tombstone reads: "Here lies Salvino d'Armato of the Armati of

Florence, inventor of spectacles. God pardon him his sins. A.D. 1317."

Meanwhile, spectacles had been invented independently in China, some time in the thirteenth century or perhaps even earlier. The Western world did not learn about this invention until 1296, when the noted adventurer Marco Polo began to write about his travels to China. He described magnifying glasses made mainly of rock crystal; the Chinese of that time were also using dark glasses made of smoky quartz.

These East Asian spectacles from the end of the eighteenth century were held on by cords looped around the ears.

It was in northern Italy, though, that glass lenses first came into their own; by the beginning of the four-teenth century, Venice had become a well-known center for optical glass considered high quality by the standards of the time.

Throughout the 1300s and the early 1400s, very few people wore glasses. There were several reasons for this. First of all, the early glasses were helpful only to *farsighted* people, those who could see things at a distance well enough but could not focus clearly on things close to them. Difficulty in close focusing is a condition that tends to increase with age (for reasons that will be discussed in a later chapter), mainly after forty or so. But in the Middle Ages the average person did not have a very good chance of living long enough to develop serious problems of this kind. In addition, not many activities of that time required really sharp close vision. One was sewing, particularly the fine needlepoint used in making tapestries. Another activity that demanded sharp close vision was reading. But since books had to be laboriously copied out by hand, few copies were available. Very few people knew how to read them, anyway. Books and scholars were found mainly in the churches and monasteries, and church-men were the earliest and most enthusiastic eyeglass wearers. Wealthy churchmen, that is: The early eye-glasses were handmade and very expensive, and only the rich could afford them. Gradually, eyeglasses be-came a status symbol. Members of the nobility wore them to impress others with their wealth or intelligence. In fact, some wealthy people who had perfectly good eyesight wore frames without lenses, just for show.

The invention of the printing press in the mid-fifteenth century, along with the development of a way to make inexpensive paper, changed all that. Books could be produced in quantity, relatively cheaply, so that even the common people could own some. More and more people learned to read, and many of them discovered that their vision was not good enough to make out the tiny printed letters without an artificial aid. The demand for eyeglasses grew, and so did the numbers of eyeglass makers. In various European countries, these craftsmen formed guilds to control the quality of the lenses. Eyeglasses that did not meet the guild standards were destroyed.

The early eyeglasses were made from glass or from transparent stones, such as beryl, quartz, or crystal. The lenses were round, and they were held in frames of metal, horn, or bone. Sometimes a single lens was used as a magnifier, held up in front of the eye by a handle. Eyeglasses with two lenses, fastened together at the appropriate distance to cover both eyes by means of a rigid connector called a *bridge*, were even more convenient. But they, too, had to be held with a handle, or balanced carefully on the nose.

The need for holding eyeglasses more securely on the face became acute in the early 1500s, when lenses for *nearsighted* people were invented. Nearsighted people can see things close to them fairly clearly, but they have trouble focusing on things at a distance—recognizing people across a room or making out a moving object far down the road. In the sixteenth century, Pope Leo X wore the new eyeglasses for hunting and was delighted at how much they improved his aim. Unlike the farsighted, who use glasses for reading or other close work, nearsighted people need to wear their eyeglasses nearly all the time. Having to hold a handle or continually grab for a pair of lenses that are toppling off the bridge of the nose can be a real nuisance. Various devices to keep glasses on were tried, including leather straps, cords that tied around the ears or had weights on the ends hanging down behind the ears, and even metal spikes that attached to the wearer's hat.

In the 1600s the rigid bridge that held the two lenses together was replaced by a spring that clamped the frames of the lenses firmly against the bridge of the nose. This style was called the *pince-nez*, which means "pinch nose" in French. As its name implies, it is effective but not very comfortable. The pince-nez remained popular, however, well into the twentieth century. Another seventeenth-century style that was popular for quite a while was the *monocle*, a single lens that was held in place in front of one eye by contractions of the facial muscles.

Eyeglass design took a giant step closer to the modern form around 1728, when Edward Scarlett, an eyeglass maker in London, invented the *temple pieces*. These steel side pieces fitted snugly along the wearer's

A portrait of astronomer Sir John Herschel from 1797 shows a loop device for holding spectacles in position; but by the nineteenth century, hand-held eyeglasses like the "quizzing glass" shown in the caricature were still in fashion.

temples and held the glasses on by pressing against the head. Later variations of temple pieces were longer and hooked behind the ears. Hinges were added to permit the glasses to be folded for convenient carrying. George Washington had a pair of eyeglasses with hinged temple pieces. (His glasses, incidentally, were imported from Europe and cost seventy-five dollars, at a time when a person could buy a full-course meal for a quarter!)

While eyeglass-frame designs were slowly being improved over the centuries, progress was also being made in lenses. Oval lenses, introduced in Europe in 1510, permitted a person to look over the lenses of reading glasses to get a clear view of things at a distance. The eighteenth century brought the invention of *bifocals*, a combination of two lenses—the lower one for reading and the upper one for distance vision. Benjamin Franklin wrote about his "double spectacles" in 1784 and was for a long time considered the inventor of bifocals. In fact, however, the idea of combining two lenses was suggested back in 1716 by C. Hertel, and London eyeglass makers were experimenting with bifocals as early as 1760.

The idea of contact lenses, which could correct vision without any cumbersome frames, dates all the way back to the Renaissance genius Leonardo da Vinci, who dreamed them up in 1508. The lenses themselves remained only a dream until 1888, when a Swiss doctor, A. Eugen Fick, and an eyeglass maker in Paris, Edouard Kalt, independently invented two different kinds of contact lenses. These were essentially glass bubbles that fitted over the entire front of the eyeball; they were very uncomfortable and could be tolerated for only a few hours at most. This type of corrective lens did not really become popular until plastics were invented.

The first plastic contact lenses were made in 1936 by William Feinbloom, a New York optometrist. They consisted of an opaque portion of molded plastic resin

Benjamin Franklin wasn't the first inventor of bifocals, but he wrote about his own "double spectacles."

that fitted over the *sclera* (the white of the eye), with a transparent glass "window" over the *cornea*, at the front of the eyeball. The hard contact lenses still in use today are made from a tough plastic, polymethyl methacrylate (PMMA), originally developed for aircraft windows and adapted to scleral lenses in 1938.

By 1939, Hollywood moviemakers were using contact lenses to change the color of actors' eyes or to produce other special effects such as the appearance of aging or even bizarre designs for extraterrestrial aliens.

Today's corneal lenses date back to prototypes developed in 1948 by an American lens technician, Kevin Tuohy, who had started out in a job program for the physically disabled because of his own severe vision problem. For a long time the only contact lenses available were hard lenses, which rigidly held their specially fitted shape. In the late 1950s, a Czech chemist, Otto Wichterle, invented a soft, water-absorbing plastic that seemed suitable for contact lenses. After a series of developments, soft lenses were put on the market by the American optical manufacturer Bausch & Lomb in 1971. Since then, the popularity of contacts has increased. According to a 1986 estimate by the Contact Lens Institute, twenty-three million Americans are wearing contact lenses—close to 10 percent of the population.

If you need corrective eyewear, you can choose from a variety of optical devices that have been refined over more than seven centuries. Before exploring the kinds of eyewear, what they do, and how you can determine which is best for you, we need some background information about nature's own vision system, the eye, how it works, and the ways it can go wrong.

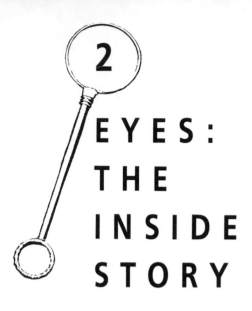

EYES: THE INSIDE STORY

2

WHEN YOU LOOK at yourself in the mirror, you can see only about one sixth of each of your eyes. For an eye is not just the colored circle with a round black center that moves about as you look at things. This colored portion is only the front part of a much larger structure, the *eyeball*.

Each eyeball looks a bit like a big round marble, about 1 inch in diameter. It is not a perfect sphere: It is somewhat longer than it is wide, with a definite bulge in the front. And unlike a marble, the eyeball is not solid all the way through; it is a tough-walled bag, filled with fluids.

The eyeball is a delicate and very important structure. Much of the information we receive about the

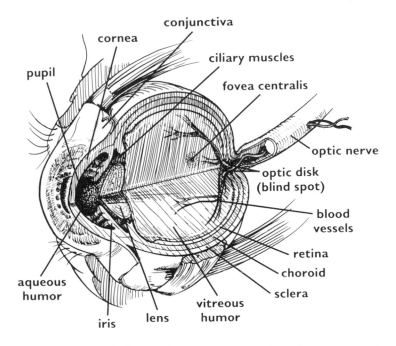

The human eyeball, partly cut away to show its structure in cross-section.

world around us comes to us through our eyes. The eyes must therefore be well protected from injury and yet open to the incoming information.

The eyeballs are well protected indeed. Each one is set deep inside a bony hollow, the *eye socket,* formed by some of the bones of the skull. The socket is lined with a thick, cushiony pad of fatty tissue, and the eyeball is suspended in a sling of muscles. (The actual

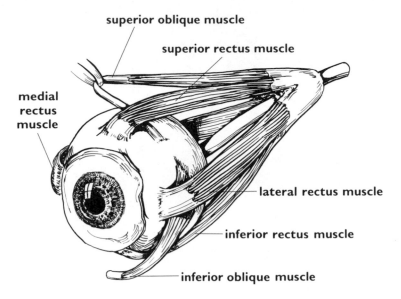

The eyeball is held in position and moved by a sling of six muscles. They are named according to the way they pull: the rectus *muscles pull straight on their point of attachment when they contract, and the* oblique *muscles exert an indirect pull.*

eyeball takes up only one fifth of the eye socket.) Bony ridges stick out above the eyes to form a projecting shelf that helps to keep things from falling into them. The stiff, bristly *eyebrows* that decorate the outsides of these ridges provide shade for the eyes and catch drops of sweat rolling down the forehead. The *eyelids*, fleshy flaps over the front of the eyes, can be drawn back into folds to expose the information-gathering part of the eyes. If the light is too bright, they can be lowered partway, acting as convenient shades. And if something threatens the eyes—like an insect or a particle of grit—the eyelids clap together tightly. This closing of the eyelids is an automatic reaction, occurring before you have time to think about it. The saying "quicker than the blink of an eye" suggests how fast the reaction is.

You may think that you don't blink very often. Actually, unless your eyes are closed, you blink between six and thirty times each minute. These unconscious blinks are not all aimed at protecting you from dive-bombing insects or other threatening objects. They work as pumps, squeezing out a bit of fluid from the *tear glands* and then spreading it evenly over the eyeball surface. We usually think of tears as just salty water, but in fact the tear film that covers the eyes has a rather complex, three-layered structure. The outermost layer is an oily substance produced by small glands at the edge of the eyelids. It helps to keep the tear fluid from evaporating. The innermost layer, consisting of mucus, is formed in the *conjunctiva*, a delicate membrane lining the inside of the eyelids and covering the surface of the eyeball. The mucus helps the tear film to spread smoothly and evenly over the eyeball. Sandwiched between these outer and inner layers is a watery fluid produced in small tear glands in the conjunctiva of the eyelid and also in a much larger *lacrimal gland* above the eye. The watery tears contain a mixture of salts, proteins, and even a bacteria-killing enzyme. After washing over the surface of the eye, the tears drain into a *tear sac* and down into the nose. Normally, just enough tear fluid is produced to keep the surface of the eye moist and wash away germs and dust particles. But an irritant (like a cold wind or a speck in your eye) or a very emotional event can make you cry, producing so many tears that they overflow the eyelids and spill out, running down your cheeks.

Front view of the eye, showing the positions of the tear glands and ducts.

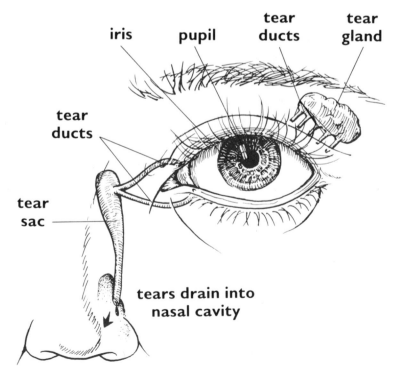

Inside the Eyeball

The eyeball has a rather complex structure. First of all, its outer wall is three layered, and each layer has an important and specialized job.

The outermost layer is tough and strong, reinforced with microscopic fibers. Above five sixths of this fibrous covering is the *sclera*, which is solid white. The rest of the outer layer—the one sixth at the front of the eyeball—is the round, transparent *cornea*, which is like a window, the only part of the outer layer that permits light rays to pass through. The cornea is also tough and strong (like the "horny" material for which it was named in Latin). When you look at a person's eyes, you see the round corneas, surrounded by white areas (the "whites of the eyes"); these are parts of the sclera.

The cornea, by the way, can be repaired if the damage (a scratch, for example) is minor. But this outer transparent window of the eye is unique in another way: Unlike the other living tissues of the body, the cornea has no direct blood supply. It must depend for nourishment on the blood vessels surrounding the junction of the cornea and sclera, the *aqueous humor* (see below), tears, and the oxygen of the air.

Unlike the cornea, the whole eye is not transparent. Looking through the cornea, you can see a colored portion of the middle layer of the eyeball wall. This is the *iris*. Its color comes from a brownish pigment, *melanin*, which may also be found in hair and skin.

Surprisingly, the same brown pigment can account for the whole range of normal eye colors, from the palest blue to the darkest black. Blue-eyed people have melanin only at the back surface of the iris. Their eyes look blue because you are seeing the dark background through a relatively clear iris. Gray, green, or hazel eyes are the result of small amounts of pigment scattered through the iris. When there is a great deal of pigment throughout the iris, eyes look brown or black. An albino's eyes are pink, because there is no pigment to cover the pinkish reflection of blood flowing through tiny vessels deeper in the eye.

The outer edge of the iris is fastened to the cornea, where the cornea and sclera meet, forming a cavity between the cornea and the iris. Watery fluid called the aqueous humor keeps this cavity firmly filled, causing the front of the eye to bulge outward.

There is a hole in the center of each iris that resembles a black circle, as you can see when you look in the mirror. This opening, the *pupil*, permits light rays to enter the eye. The size of the pupil can vary greatly. This is easy to demonstrate by shining a flashlight into one eye as you look at yourself in the mirror. Your pupil promptly narrows (*constricts*) in response to the brighter light. Curiously enough, the pupils of both eyes constrict, even if the light shines into only one of them. This is an automatic reaction, which protects the eyes from too bright a light. When lights are dim, the pupils widen (*dilate*), again automatically, to allow more light to enter. This automatic adjustment of the pupillary openings makes vision possible over a wide range of light intensities.

The size of the pupil is controlled by two sets of muscles in the iris. One set, which radiates outward like the spokes of a wheel, causes the pupil to dilate when the muscle fibers contract. The other set of muscles consists of circular fibers, which cause the pupil to constrict when they contract, narrowing the round opening like the action of purse strings drawing a bag

The size of the pupil is controlled by the action of two sets of muscles in the iris: radial *muscles produce dilation, and* circular *(sphincter) muscles draw in like purse strings when they contract, constricting the pupil.*

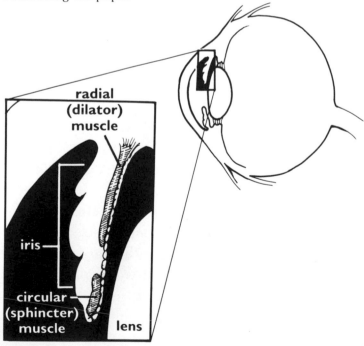

radial (dilator) muscle

iris—

circular— (sphincter) muscle

lens

closed. This type of purse-string muscle is called a *sphincter muscle.*

Researchers have discovered that the muscles regulating the size of the pupil are also partly controlled by the emotions. When you are reading something very interesting, your pupils tend to widen. For example, you may find the tiny beam of a penlight perfectly adequate for reading that exciting mystery story you smuggled under the covers to read late at night, whereas a good desk lamp may not seem to be providing enough light to read a dull assignment. When young men are shown photos of attractive women, their pupils dilate. Women show a similar reaction when they see a photo of a baby. Both sexes show a unique reaction to a picture of something frightening or gruesome, like a photo of a bad car crash: First the pupils dilate, and then they quickly constrict, as though trying to shut out the sight.

Certain drugs can also affect the size of the pupils. Narcotics such as morphine and heroin produce extremely constricted, "pinpoint" pupils. Cocaine stimulates the muscles of the iris to dilate the pupils. Atropine, a drug extracted from a plant of the deadly nightshade family, produces the same effect by temporarily paralyzing the constricting muscles. Another name for this drug, belladonna ("beautiful lady" in Italian), comes from the fact that women used to put drops of the drug in their eyes to make themselves look more attractive. (Presumably a man would find a woman with dilated pupils attractive because she would seem interested in him.)

At the back of the eyeball, the middle layer of the wall (under the sclera) is called the *choroid*. This part of the three-layered wall has a rich supply of blood vessels and a dark pigment that prevents light rays from being reflected and bouncing around inside the eyeball. At the front edge of the choroid, where it meets the iris, is a thickened ring—the *ciliary body*. Much of this structure is made up of muscles, which are attached to the bandlike ligaments that suspend the *lens*. The term lens comes from "lentil," a kind of bean, and is a rough description of its shape. It hangs behind the iris, held firmly in place by muscles and ligaments and positioned so that the pupil is approximately lined up with its center. The lens thus forms the back wall of the chamber, under the cornea, filled with the watery fluid called the aqueous humor. ("Aqueous" means watery in Latin.)

The lens is a transparent structure. Unlike the glass or plastic lenses of eyewear, it is only semisolid. It consists of long fibers, arranged in sheets like the layers of an onion and held together by a thin, elastic membrane. When the ringlike ciliary muscle is relaxed, the pull on the suspending ligaments gives the lens a somewhat flattened shape. When the muscle contracts, the ring narrows and the pull on the ligaments is reduced. The lens balloons out, becoming more spherical and changing the way light rays pass through it.

The lens of the eye must last a lifetime, for the body cannot repair or replace it. A baby's lens is almost spherical, but with age it gradually flattens out, loses water, and becomes more dense and less elastic.

The innermost part of the eyeball's three-layered coat is the *retina*, which lines the back of the eyeball just inside the choroid. This is a light-sensitive lining that translates light rays into nerve impulses. Under a microscope, the retina is found to have a very complicated structure, consisting of ten distinct layers. Light that has entered the eye passes through each layer in turn. The next-to-last layer contains specialized cells named for their shapes: *rods* and *cones*. These are the light-receiving cells. A tiny bit of light is enough to stimulate the rods, which help us to make out shapes and movement in dim light. Brighter light is needed to stimulate the cones, of which there are three kinds; they provide for color vision. The last of the retinal layers, just under the choroid, contains a dark pigment, which prevents confusing reflections of light inside the eye.

Peering through the cornea, pupil, and lens into the interior of the eyeball, the eye doctor can see two important landmarks on the dark background of the retina. Near the center there is a small, oval, yellowish spot, the *macula lutea* (Latin for "yellow spot"). At the center of the macula lutea is a little hollow, where the retina is thinner. This is the *fovea centralis*, the spot where vision is clearest and sharpest. When you read, your eyes move continually, shifting to bring the

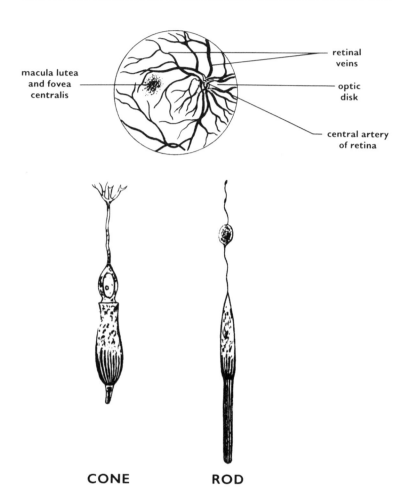

macula lutea
and fovea
centralis

retinal
veins

optic
disk

central artery
of retina

CONE   **ROD**

A view of the retina at the back of the eye, as it is seen through the cornea, pupil, and lens, is shown at the top. A cone and a rod, the specialized vision cells, are shown highly magnified at the bottom.

rays of light from each word to focus on the fovea.

The other prominent landmark on the retina, the *optic disk*, lies about 2 millimeters from the macula lutea, on the side toward the nose. This is the point where nerve fibers from the retina merge to form the *optic nerve*, which passes out through the back of the eyeball and carries sensory messages from the retina to the brain. There are no rods or cones at all in that spot on the retina, so any light rays that happen to fall on it will not be registered. The optic disk is thus a "blind spot." Normally there are not any spots missing from what you see, because the sensory information from the two eyes, together with continual shifting movements of the eyes, provide enough information to fill in the blanks. But there are some easy ways to demonstrate your own blind spot.

For example, look at the simple diagram on page 27. Covering your left eye, hold the page up about a foot from you and stare at the X with your right eye. Then move the page closer or farther away until the dot seems to disappear. At that point, the light rays from the dot are falling on the optic disk, the "blind spot" of your eye.

Another way to experience the blind spot is to place seven coins in a row on a table, about 6 or 8 inches from your face. Now close your left eye and stare at the coin in the center with your right eye. One of the coins on the right side seems to disappear! When you close your right eye and stare at the center coin with your left, a coin on the left will vanish.

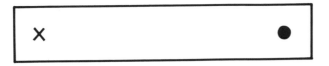

To find your "blind spot," cover your left eye and focus with the right on the cross. Then move the page closer and farther until the dot seems to disappear. At this point its image is falling on the optic disk, which lacks rods and cones.

The large rear portion of the eye, bounded by the lens and the retina, is filled with a jellylike substance. This is called the *vitreous humor*. (Vitreous means "glassy.") Making up about 80 percent of the eye, it helps to maintain the shape of the eyeball and nourishes the retina.

Now we have completed a brief exploration of the eye, but we still have only a small part of the vision story. To understand the rest, we need some simple principles of physics and a look at how the eyes work with the brain.

3
EYES AND
OPTICS:
HOW WE SEE

THE TRAILBLAZING PIONEER of the science of vision was an eleventh-century Arabian scientist named Alhazen. He suggested that light from the sun is reflected from visible objects to the eye of the observer, and the images of objects are carried to the brain by the optic nerves. Those ideas seem logical now, but they were revolutionary in the period when Alhazen worked. At that time scientific thought on the subject of vision was dominated by the theories of Pythagoras, who had stated back in the sixth century B.C. that light rays emerged from the eye and bounced off objects back into the lens.

The eleventh-century Arabian astronomer Alhazen was the first to suggest that light is reflected from an object to the eye.

The Eye as a Camera

The human eye has often been compared to a camera. In some ways that comparison is valid. An eye and a camera both have a lens, which focuses light rays and

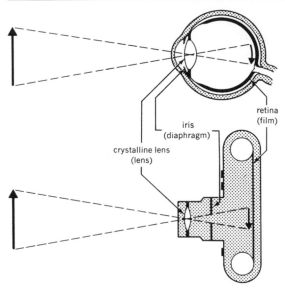

The working eye has some similarities to a camera.

produces an image of external objects. The camera shutter, which opens to admit light to the lens or shuts to block it out, is comparable to the eyelids. The amount of light that reaches a camera lens when the shutter is open is controlled by an adjustable diaphragm, which widens or narrows the aperture (opening) just as the muscles of the iris dilate or constrict the pupil of the eye.

In a camera the image is focused onto a film coated with light-sensitive chemicals; *photochemical* reactions ("photo" means "light") in the coating produce dark and light areas, depending on the strength of the light striking each point. In the eye the image is focused onto the light-sensitive retina, producing photochemical reactions in the rods and cones that define the light and dark areas of the image. For reasons that will become clear a little later, the image produced on the camera film and that on the retina are both upside down.

But now the comparison begins to break down. A single print is made from a photonegative, whereas the image on the retina is converted by the stimulated rods and cones to a collection of nerve impulses. These signals are carried to the brain. In this respect, the eye is more like a video recorder than a simple camera. Like the video recorder, it produces not just single photos but a continuous series of images, which the brain processes into a smooth-flowing "motion picture."

Some Simple Optics

Optics is the science of light and vision. *Light* is a form of electromagnetic radiation that can be thought of as traveling in waves.

Light waves move very rapidly. They travel through a vacuum at a speed of about 186,000 miles per second. They move nearly as rapidly in air and other gases, although they travel more slowly in liquids and solids. In general, the denser a substance is, the more slowly light travels through it. The ratio of the speed of light in air to its speed in a substance defines the *refractive index* of the substance. Air itself has a refractive index very close to 1.00; for various kinds of glass the values range from 1.50 to 1.9; and the index for water is about 1.33.

A *light ray* is a kind of charting of the path of the traveling light waves. When light waves strike the surface of a different substance, with a different density, some may be *reflected* (bounced back) from the surface, and some may be transmitted through the new substance. The light rays in the diagrams on page 33 show how light is reflected or transmitted in various ways.

If the light is moving in a direction perpendicular to the surface, then it will be both reflected straight back along the same ray and transmitted through the new medium in the same direction. So the path of the light rays will still be a simple straight line. But if the light hits the surface at an angle, the direction will change. As you can see from the diagram, the ray of light that is reflected will form a new angle with the surface that is exactly equal to the angle formed by the light coming in. The light that is transmitted through the new medium will be bent or *refracted*, abruptly changing direction at the surface.

As we have noted, a *lens* is a transparent object that changes the path of light rays—that is, refracts them. It may cause the rays to *converge* (move toward each other, eventually meeting at a point) or *diverge* (move away from each other). A lens is typically described according to the shape of its surface. A surface that is perfectly flat is called *plano*; one that curves outward is *convex*; and one that curves inward (like

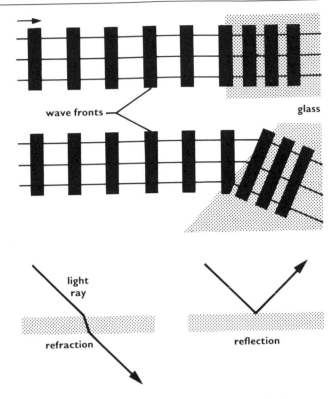

Some basic optics. When the light rays enter glass, the distance between wave fronts gets shorter. When a light ray hits a boundary between two different substances, such as air and glass, it may be refracted or reflected—or both.

a bowl) is *concave.* The lens of the human eye, with both sides curving outward, is thus *biconvex.* Glass or plastic lenses can be ground in a variety of shapes: biconvex, *biconcave* (both surfaces curving inward), *concave-convex, planoconvex* (one surface flat, the other curving outward), *planoconcave.*

As you can see from the diagrams on page 34, different types of lenses have different effects on light rays. Let's consider what happens when light rays strike a biconvex lens.

Light rays coming from a distant source can be considered as parallel. Those that strike the center of the lens are perpendicular to its surface and thus are transmitted straight through, without changing the direction of their path. But the light rays that strike

A biconvex lens converges parallel light rays to a focal point; a biconcave lens causes light rays to diverge, so that there is no real focus.

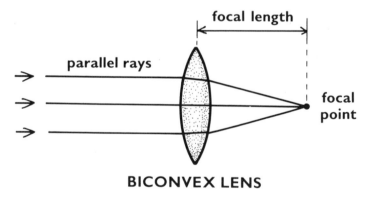

BICONVEX LENS

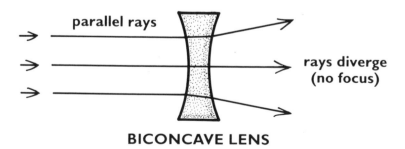

BICONCAVE LENS

points farther out toward the edges hit the surface of the lens at an angle. These rays are bent inward. (The farther out from the center, the greater the refraction.) The whole beam of parallel rays is finally converged into a single point, which is called the *focus* or *focal point*. The distance from the lens to the focal point is called the *focal length*. The *refractive power* of a lens is measured in units called *diopters*, equal to one divided by the focal length of the lens expressed in meters. A bioconcave lens diverges light rays, and thus it has no real focus. (Its focal length can be computed by charting the rays backward to the single point from which they seem to be emerging. This point is called a *virtual focus*.)

Optics and the Eyes

The biconvex lens of the human eye converges light rays to a focal point, just like a glass or plastic lens with a similar shape. But the lens is not the only refracting medium in the eye. Entering light rays pass through the cornea, aqueous humor, lens, and vitreous humor before they finally reach the retina. Each of these has its own refractive index: the cornea 1.38, aqueous humor 1.33, lens 1.40, and vitreous humor 1.34. So the light rays striking the surface of the cornea are bent and bent again as they thread their way through the pupil and into the interior of the eye. All these refractions must be taken into account. All together, the refracting system of the human eye has a focal length of 16.7 millimeters, which is about the distance from the lens to the retina in a normal eyeball. In other words, the laws of optics predict that incoming light rays will be nicely focused right onto the retina. The refractive power of the eye ranges from about 60 to 75 diopters.

In the example of a biconvex lens, we considered the case of a distant light source, whose rays can be thought of as parallel. Light rays from a close source, though, diverge, spreading out as they approach the eye. Such rays can be focused by a biconvex lens too, but they must be bent inward more to be focused onto the same spot—that is, onto the retina. The adjustable shape of the eye lens allows for focusing both nearby objects and far-off scenes.

Tracing the paths of light rays from several different points on the cornea through the refracting media of the eye to the retina yields a rather surprising result. As the illustration on page 37 shows, the image formed on the retina is *inverted*. And yet you don't see things upside down. That is because your brain automatically corrects the upside-down images from the retina. This ability is something we all learn from experience, as babies. Further experiences can change the way we "see" things. In one experiment, volunteers wore special distorting spectacles that inverted everything they saw. At first, things seemed to be upside-down, with tables and chairs resting on the ceiling and people standing on their heads. But within a few days the

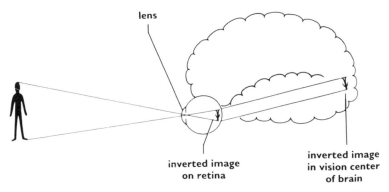

Light rays focused by the refracting systems of the eye produce a reduced, upside-down image on the retina. This image is transmitted by the optic nerve to the vision center at the back of the brain.

volunteers' brains relearned their way of looking at things and "saw" everything right side up again. (When the volunteers took the special glasses off, they had another few days of adjustment as their brains relearned the old set of inverting rules.)

There is another difference between a real object and its image on the retina: The retinal image is *reduced*. That is not so surprising; there is not enough room on the inch or so of retinal surface to project, for example, a 6-foot image of a 6-foot man. The size of the image depends not only on the size of the object but also on the distance from the object to the eyes: More distant objects look smaller than closer ones that are actually the same size. This apparent size difference, depending on the distance, is called *perspective*. It provides clues to depth perception that the

brain uses in interpreting what the eyes see. Size differences are used as cues to estimate relative distances.
Artists take advantage of perspective to fool the brain
and give a three-dimensional look to flat, two-dimen-
sional drawings. By making nearby objects much larger,
relatively, than distant ones, they give an illusion of
depth.

More about Vision

In a simple box camera, the shutter speed, size of the
aperture (opening to the lens), and distance of the lens
from the film are all fixed. As a result, the kinds of
pictures this camera can take are rather limited. Objects at a certain distance come out sharp and clear
in the photos, but distant things and close-ups are just
a blur. If the light is too dim, the pictures will be dark,
while too bright a light can produce a washed-out,
overexposed effect. More complex cameras provide
various options. You can change the shutter speed and
aperture (or the camera may even do it for you, according to the readings of a built-in light meter). Also,
the lens is mounted on a movable framework, so that
its distance from the film can be changed to bring
different parts of the scene into sharp focus. The human
eye is even better—comparable to a complicated camera hooked up to a computer that continuously adjusts
the apertures and lens systems according to the light

conditions; and it can zoom in on an interesting detail or scan the distant horizon.

The "computer" hooked up to the human eyes is the brain. Whenever a rod or cone is stimulated, a tiny electrical message is relayed along nerve fibers that extend from the retina through the optic nerve to the brain. There are two eyes, thus two optic nerves, and also two main areas in the brain specialized for processing visual information. These visual centers are found at the back of the brain. If you "see stars" after bumping the back of your head, that is because the main vision area of the brain has been stimulated directly, just as though a very strong message had come in from the optic nerves.

When you focus a camera, you change the distance from the lens to the film, so that the focus of the image will fall on the light-sensitive area. The human eye has only very limited capabilities for making that kind of adjustment. Although the lens moves slightly forward or back when the muscles suspending it contract, the change in its distance to the retina is not usually enough to bring the image into clear focus. Instead, light rays from different distances are converged onto the retina by changing the shape of the lens and thus changing its focal length. This change in the curve of the lens is called *accommodation*. It is a reflex action; when you are looking at a close object, the ciliary muscle automatically contracts, drawing the ciliary body forward and decreasing the pull on the ligaments

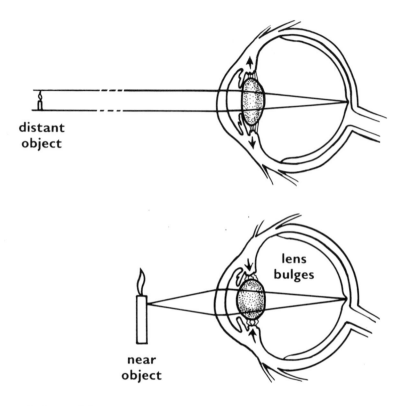

distant
object

lens
bulges

near
object

The lens of the eye can change its shape to accommodate a close
object. The rounder shape bends the light rays more sharply so
that they converge to a focus on the retina.

holding the lens. As a result, the lens bulges, becoming more convex, and its refracting power increases.
When you are looking at a distant object, circular fibers in the ciliary muscle relax and radial fibers contract;
both actions make the ligaments pull harder on the lens, flattening it and decreasing its refracting power.

Your two eyes view the same scene from slightly different positions in the face, and therefore they send slightly different pictures to the brain. The brain puts all this information together to produce a *stereoscopic* image, which provides an impression of distance and depth. This *binocular* (two-eyed) vision is coordinated by the brain through movements of the eyeballs. The muscular sling that holds the eyeball suspended in its bony socket includes six different muscles, whose different pulls can combine to move the eyeball up, down, left, or right. When these movements are not perfectly coordinated, and the images do not fall on corresponding points in the retinas of the two eyes, the result is *diplopia* (double vision).

In merging the images of the two eyes, one eye tends to dominate, and the scene is observed as though you were looking out from that eye. To determine which of your eyes is *dominant*, look across the room and pick out a particular spot on the wall. Now raise one finger far from your face and hold it so that it covers the spot. Holding the finger steady, close first one eye, then the other. When you are looking through your dominant eye, there will seem to be no change, and your finger will still be covering the spot. But if you close that eye and look through the other, your finger will seem to jump aside and no longer will cover the spot. Usually (but not always) the dominant eye is on the same side of the body as the dominant hand. So if you are right-handed, you will probably be right-eyed, too. Curiously, a study has shown that more than 50 percent of major-league baseball players have *crossed dominance*—right-handed and left-eyed, for example—compared to only 20 percent of the general population. For a batter, crossed dominance is an advantage: When he is in the batting stance that favors the strength of his dominant hand, his dominant eye is in the best position to follow the flight of the ball.

Most of what we have been saying about eyes and how they work holds true for normal eyes. But some eyes do not have the right shape or proportions or muscle action to focus images clearly. In the following chapters we will find out how manufactured lenses, in the form of eyeglasses or contact lenses, can help to correct vision problems.

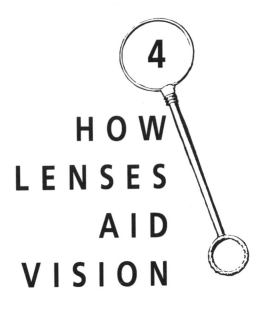

4

HOW
LENSES
AID
VISION

IN THE LAST CHAPTER we mentioned that the shape of the lens and the proportions of the human eye are just right for focusing light rays onto the retina. That is the case for a normal eye. But eyes, like other human traits, vary. Just as some people may be tall and skinny and others short and fat, eyeballs may be longer or shorter than the average; or there may be variations in the curvature of the cornea. Although the eye muscles permit a substantial variation of the shape of the lens, this may not be enough to compensate. No matter how hard the eye tries, it may be simply impossible to focus images onto the retina.

That is where corrective lenses come in. For the most common vision defects, lenses can be devised to change the direction of the incoming light rays just enough so that the refractions in the eye produce a clear image on the retina. Different types of vision problems call for various kinds of corrective lenses.

Myopia

If you can see close objects fairly well, but things at a distance are a blur, your vision problem is called nearsightedness, or *myopia*. Like the cartoon character Mr. Magoo, the myope may not recognize peo-

The nearsighted eye is unable to converge light rays from a distant object to a clear focus on the retina. The refraction can be corrected with a concave lens.

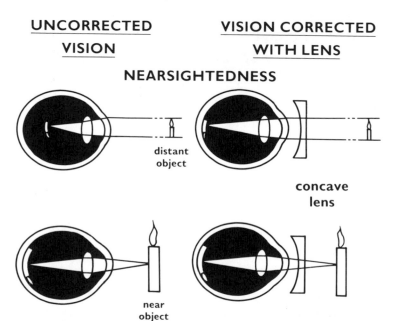

UNCORRECTED VISION   **VISION CORRECTED WITH LENS**

NEARSIGHTEDNESS

distant object

concave lens

near object

ple across the room or may even mistake lampposts or other objects for people. A myope driving a car without wearing glasses is a sure prescription for disaster. (It is also illegal.) Yet the nearsighted person may be able to read quite easily without glasses.

Several different conditions can result in myopia. If the eyeball is longer than normal, the focal point of light rays from distant objects may fall short of the retina. No matter how hard the ciliary muscles try to adjust the shape of the lens, they may not be able to change it enough to compensate. Too much curvature in the lens or cornea might also cause myopia by refracting the light rays so much that, again, the focal point falls short of the retina. A similar result may occur if the inner parts of the eye have too great a refracting power.

In all these conditions, although distant objects appear blurry, it may be possible to see close objects clearly: The light rays coming from them are diverging as they reach the eye (not parallel, like the rays from distant objects). The longer distance inside the eyeball or the extra refraction may be just enough to focus these diverging rays onto the retina.

Myopia can be corrected with a biconcave or planoconcave lens. The lens diverges light rays from distant objects, so they reach the cornea at an angle (just as rays from close objects do without glasses). Then the lens of the eye is able to converge the rays to focus on the retinal surface, and a clear image is formed.

Myopic people need to wear their corrective lenses

for most ordinary activities, such as sports, driving, or even walking across the room. But they may have to take the glasses off for reading or close work (or switch to a pair of reading glasses). Another alternative is to use bifocals that provide for both near and far vision.

Myopia is fairly easy to diagnose, and it is usually caught early in life. A child who needs to sit in the front row in order to see the blackboard soon comes

Myopia is often diagnosed in childhood.

to the teacher's attention. After routine eye tests in
school, using the standard wall eye chart, many children are sent home with a note recommending a visit
to an eye doctor. Teenagers who are a bit nearsighted
may fail the eye test for a driver's license, which is
geared toward distance vision.

When a child is myopic, the nearsightedness tends
to increase with age, up to about the age of twenty,
when growth is basically completed. Health statistics
suggest that the number of cases of myopia among
the population is increasing. These observations have
caused some concern and a great deal of controversy
about what causes myopia and what should be done
about it.

Some specialists claim that our modern civilization,
with its emphasis on close work—for example, reading and work on computer terminals—is causing more
myopia. According to one theory, overworking the
eyes for long periods of time, especially with the head
downward (as in leaning over a desk), increases the
fluid pressure inside the eye and causes the eyeball to
enlarge. But most children who put in the same reading effort don't become myopic, so it seems that he-
redity may also play an important role: A particular
type of eye stress might produce myopia only in children who are born with the tendency.

Other eye specialists believe that many of the children diagnosed as myopic are not really nearsighted
at all. Instead, they suffer from *pseudomyopia*, a condition in which poor distance vision is the result of

"cramps" in the eye-focusing muscles. After a long session of close work, these muscles are so tense that they cannot relax fully when the eyes look at something far away. This kind of muscle cramping can even make farsighted eyes seem myopic, but there are ways of testing vision that can distinguish the "false myopia" from the real condition.

Hyperopia

Hyperopia (farsightedness) is the reverse of myopia. A farsighted person can see things at a distance better than those close by. The cause is an eyeball that is shorter than normal, so that the focal point of light rays from a close object falls behind the retina. No adjustment of the lens by the ciliary muscles can compensate enough to bring the image into focus on the retinal surface. The lens cannot converge the rays enough. But the light rays from a distant object do not need as much refraction, and it may be possible to focus them clearly. So the hyperope may be able to see objects at a distance well enough—even to read street signs a block away—while the printed words of a book, held at the normal reading distance, are just a blur.

Not all farsighted people can see clearly at a distance; their eyes may not even be able to converge the light rays from a distant object. But their distance

FARSIGHTEDNESS

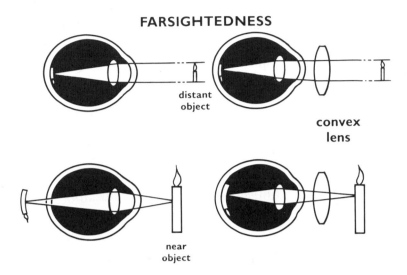

The farsighted eye is unable to converge light rays from a close object to a clear focus on the retina. The refractions can be corrected with a convex lens.

vision is better than their near vision.

Some children with hyperopia may unconsciously attempt to see close objects more clearly by using the muscles outside the eyeball to turn one or both eyes inward toward the bridge of the nose. (Normally, both eyes move in unison: When one turns to the left, the other turns an equal amount to the left as well.) When one or both eyes turn inward, the child has a *cross-eyed* appearance. Eye specialists refer to this condition as *convergent strabismus*, or *accommodative estropia*. Children with myopia may develop a different type of eye-turning abnormality: *divergent strabismus*, which produces a *wall-eyed* appearance—one or both eyes turn outward. The failure of the eyes to coordinate their movements normally may result in blurred or double vision. In both kinds of strabismus, after a while, the child may learn to "turn off" the messages from one eye and get a clearer picture (but without normal depth perception) by using just the other. Eventually, the unused eye may become unable to see at all, a condition called *lazy eye* or *amblyopia*. In some cases, strabismus can be corrected simply by wearing a pair of glasses that corrects the underlying vision problem. (Sometimes glasses may be prescribed to keep the eyes straight even though the patient can see clearly without the corrective lenses.) In other cases, special exercises, patching of one eye, and even surgery may be needed. (This will be discussed in more detail in Chapter 8.)

Hyperopia can be corrected with a biconvex lens, which adds converging power to the eye's own natural refracting system. The person may need to wear the corrective lenses all the time, for both near and distant vision. Or only reading glasses for close work may be necessary. Bifocals may furnish an appropriate correction for near vision in the lower lens, combined with upper lenses that either give no magnification at all (plano) or provide the correction needed for distance vision. Their great convenience is that one does not have to continually take glasses off and put them on again.

Presbyopia

In their mid-forties, even people who have never had any vision problems may gradually become "farsighted." *Presbyopia*, which literally means "old sight," is a special kind of farsightedness. The problem is not that the eyeball is too short—as in hyperopia—but rather that the lens can no longer do the necessary work of focusing. With age the lens of the eye gradually becomes flatter and less elastic, and the ciliary muscles may grow flabby and weak. Accommodation becomes more and more difficult. Although the light rays from a close object theoretically could still be focused onto the retina, the effort to do so is a strain, and the eye muscles may just give up.

The saying that "you know you need glasses when your arms get too short to read" has a lot of truth in it. A presbyopic person tends to hold reading materials farther out than normal, seeking unconsciously to put the print at a distance where the letters can be comfortably brought into sharp focus. As time goes by, the distance between eyes and print gets longer, until finally "the arms are too short." (One of us, long used to the pleasures of effortless reading and close work, did not realize she had grown presbyopic until someone remarked, "Why are you holding your book so far away?")

Presbyopia is corrected in the same way as hyperopia, with a biconvex lens. Examinations every year or two are advisable, because the loss of flexibility of

The customer of this itinerant eyeglass merchant from the end
of the eighteenth century is obviously farsighted.

the eye's accommodating system increases with age, and so does the amount of correction needed. At the age of about sixty-five or seventy, the loss of flexibility levels off, and after that little or no change in glasses is needed.

Farsighted people are affected by presbyopia at an earlier age than usual, because they are already using part of their focusing power for distance vision. Near-sighted people may be delighted to discover in middle age that they no longer need their glasses. To some degree, presbyopia may compensate for their natural myopia.

In general, though, presbyopia can be a frightening condition. Finding that the near vision is growing poorer, and stronger glasses are needed each year, a person may wonder, "Am I going blind?" The eye doctor's answer is a relief: "There's nothing wrong with your eyes except for their age." Although the near vision may continue to worsen, it can still be corrected with glasses, and one can go on reading for a lifetime.

Astigmatism

Was El Greco astigmatic? This sixteenth-century Spanish artist had a very distinctive style. In his paint-ings, people's faces and bodies are oddly elongated—not merely tall but out of normal proportion. Eye specialists today believe El Greco's unique images were

Astigmatism produces a distorted image.

the result not only of his imagination but also of a vision defect. When El Greco paintings are viewed through the kind of lens that is used to correct a common vision problem called *astigmatism*, all the people and objects suddenly look "normal."

The normal cornea has the curvature of a perfect sphere. But few people's eyes are perfect, and the cornea may be shaped more like a cone or an elongated spoon shape; or its surface may include small bulges or ripples. These deviations from the ideal spherical curve may be so minor that they make no practical difference. Or the differences in curvature may produce distortions of the image; no matter how hard they try, the lens and its muscles cannot get all parts of the image into focus at once. This kind of vision problem is called astigmatism. (The root "stigma" means "spot" in Latin, and in this condition there is literally no spot at which the light rays from all parts of the cornea come to a focus.)

Typically, a person with astigmatism does not realize that anything is wrong. The brain learns to compensate and views the distorted image as normal. When astigmatism is corrected with lenses, the patient typically complains for a few days that things seem tilted and out of shape. But gradually the brain adjusts and learns to see the clear image correctly. Untreated, astigmatism may cause headaches and eyestrain as the eye muscles keep trying vainly to focus.

Astigmatism is diagnosed by means of special diagrams like the one on page 56. To a person with normal vision, all the lines have the same darkness. But to someone with astigmatism, some of the lines will appear darker than others. Careful testing permits the doctor to plot the distortions of the corneal curvature. Then a special lens is designed and ground to compensate for these distortions, so that the combination of corrective lens and astigmatic cornea refracts light rays as though it were a portion of a sphere. Often cylindrical lenses are incorporated into the corrective prescription.

It is rare for both of a person's eyes to have exactly the same vision problems. While especially true of astigmatism, this can also hold true for myopia or hyperopia. The appropriate correction for each eye

To test yourself for astigmatism, hold this page at your normal reading distance. Look at the illustration first with one eye closed, then the other. If some sections of the image look blacker or sharper than others, you may have an irregularity in the curvature of the cornea (astigmatism).

must be determined separately, and the two lenses in a pair of glasses or contacts may not match. (One of us has a pair of glasses that incorporates a correction for hyperopia in one eye and for myopia in the other, with a correction for astigmatism thrown in.)

When You Need Glasses . . .

How can you tell if you have a vision problem? Obviously, if things look blurred when you try to read or to make out a face in the distance, you may need corrective lenses. But many people are so used to their vision defects that they may not realize there is any-thing wrong. (If things have appeared blurry all your life, how could you know what clear images are sup-posed to look like?) Vision screening tests in schools and in routine physical examinations may turn up a vision defect. (Myopia is more likely to be noticed in school; but children who have reading problems be-cause they cannot see the letters clearly enough may be thought to be slow learners.)

A feeling of tiredness, heaviness, burning, tearing, a sandy sensation, or pain in the eyes, which may be accompanied by headache or sensitivity to light, can be a warning signal. But the cause of such *eyestrain* may not be a vision defect. Eye fatigue or strain may also develop if you try to use your eyes when you are very tired or sleepy, suffering from a cold or other illness, or perhaps under a great emotional strain. Even lack of enough exercise can produce symptoms of eyestrain. You may think you need glasses when ac-tually all you need is to take a break and go for a walk. Trying to read in dim light or an irritating glare can also cause problems. But if eye symptoms persist, determining their cause is not a do-it-yourself project; it is a job for an expert.

5
GETTING GLASSES

FOR HUNDREDS OF YEARS, getting a pair of glasses was a hit-or-miss affair. If you were having trouble with reading or close work, you consulted a peddler or jeweler and tried on whatever spectacles were available. The glasses were marked according to the age of the prospective wearer. There was nothing scientific about the fitting of glasses—you simply chose the pair that felt most comfortable.

Many people still buy glasses in much the same way, choosing from the display in a drug or department store or sending away to a mail-order house, whose catalog might specify suggested age ranges rather than magnifying power. (Some states, including Louisiana, Kansas, Massachusetts, Minnesota, New

The Spectacle Seller's Stall *was painted by the Dutch artist Stradanus around 1530. One man is holding a single, hand-held lens, while others in the marketplace scene are wearing spectacles.*

York, and Rhode Island, have laws prohibiting the sale of over-the-counter glasses.) Such ready-made glasses have biconvex lenses providing simple magnification for farsightedness, and the magnifying powers of both lenses are the same. There is no consideration of the individual needs of each eye, nor any help for people with myopia or astigmatism.

Even if all you need is simple magnification, the same for both eyes, you are still better off having your eyes examined regularly by a professional. This specialist will not only determine the proper prescription but also routinely check your eyes for various diseases. This is an important benefit: Some conditions, unless caught and treated early, can lead to blindness. (An increase in the pressure inside the eyeball, for example, might be a warning sign of glaucoma.) An examination by an eye specialist is also vital if you want contact lenses, which must be precisely fitted to your eyes.

Kinds of Eye Specialists

Many people are confused about the various "O words" that designate the different eye specialists. There are two main kinds of specialists who can examine eyes and prescribe corrective lenses: ophthalmologists and optometrists.

An *ophthalmologist* is a doctor of medicine (either an M.D. or a D.O., doctor of osteopathy), who has specialized in the diagnosis and treatment of eye diseases and disorders. An ophthalmologist has completed four years of college, four years of medical school, one or more years of general hospital experience, and three or more years in a hospital-based residency program emphasizing the study of the eye and its related systems. This specialist must pass state board, national board, and specialty board examinations and then continue to study, learning about new advances in the field through graduate training courses, clinical conferences, and medical meetings. The ophthalmologist examines the eyes in relation to the general health and condition of the body and may use or prescribe medicines, glasses, contact lenses, or

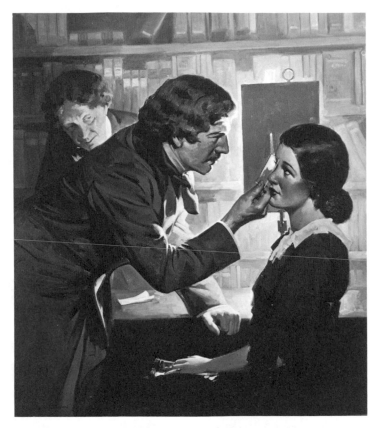

Hermann von Helmholtz is shown here examining a patient with the ophthalmoscope that he invented in 1851.

special eye exercises; he or she may also perform eye surgery.

An *optometrist* is a doctor of optometry (an O.D., not to be confused with the D.O. degree in osteopathy). An optometrist has completed two to four years of college and four years of classroom and clinical training at a school of optometry but does not have the general medical training that an ophthalmologist completes. He or she must be licensed by the state in order to practice optometry and may also be affiliated with the state optometric association. This eye specialist concentrates on eye disorders that can be treated with glasses, contact lenses, or special exercises to correct muscle imbalances. He or she also detects signs of eye disease and general health problems—such as high blood pressure or diabetes—that show up in the eyes. (People with such diseases are referred to the appropriate health professional for treatment.) In most states, optometrists are also permitted to use eye medicines for diagnosis or therapy of eye disorders.

There is also a general term, *oculist*, which can refer to either an ophthalmologist or an optometrist.

The word *optician* describes a professional who dispenses glasses and contact lenses. He or she provides, fits, and adjusts glasses, contact lenses, and other optical devices according to the written prescription of an ophthalmologist or optometrist. The optician is not a doctor; most opticians get their training on the job. Only a minority of states require formal licensing, but opticians may belong to a professional guild that maintains standards. In most areas, optometrists do not make glasses but may recommend one or more opticians who they feel are particularly skilled and accurate. An optometrist may fill prescriptions for corrective lenses in addition to prescribing them. But the patient is always free to take the prescription and have it filled by an optician of his or her choice.

How can you decide which kind of eye specialist to see, and then how can you find a good one? If you suspect you may have an eye disease, then you need to see an ophthalmologist. But if you just want a pair of glasses or contact lenses, you can choose among ophthalmologists and optometrists. There are pros and cons to each.

Ophthalmologists say that only a doctor of medicine has the knowledge and experience to give you total eye care, checking to make sure your eyes are healthy, determining whether you really need glasses, and prescribing the right kind of corrective lenses. Optometrists, though, point out that ophthalmologists have most of their training, and spend most of their practice, in diagnosing and treating eye diseases. They say that optometrists concentrate on prescribing glasses and therefore have more practice in determining the best ways to correct refraction problems. Optometrists, by the way, are trained to check for diseases and will refer you to a medical specialist if needed.

When an eye specialist only prescribes glasses, you must go to an optician to have the prescription filled. Many optometrists and some ophthalmologists are set up to provide full service, from examining and prescribing to making up and fitting the glasses or contact lenses. That can be much more convenient, but it can also be a potential conflict of interest: When the specialist makes a profit from dispensing glasses as well as prescribing them, there may be at least an uncon-

scious motivation to prescribe corrective lenses in bor-
derline cases when they may not really be needed.
How much weight should be given to all these con-
siderations is something for each individual patient to
decide.

One of the best ways to find a good eye specialist
is to get recommendations from friends or relatives
who are pleased with theirs. Or perhaps a family doctor will be familiar with the qualifications of specialists
in your area. To find out about ophthalmologists, you
can call a local hospital and ask for the names of eye
specialists on their staff; or you can call the local
medical society, which is usually listed in the telephone
book under "Medical Society of the County of . . ."
Similarly, a call to your state optometric society, listed
under the name of the state (for example, "New Jersey
Optometric Society"), will get you a list of names and
addresses of reliable optometrists in your area. If your
family is covered under a program of health insurance
benefits, the program may provide a list of partici-
pating optometrists or ophthalmologists.

Once you have selected an eye specialist, the examination itself will give you some idea of whether
you wish to go back to the same person later.

The Eye Examination

The first step in a vision examination is an interview.
The doctor will want to know what your problem
is—whether you are just in for a routine exam or have

some particular vision difficulty. Information on your general health history and that of your family may provide important clues for diagnosing eye problems and may alert the doctor to watch for symptoms of diseases, such as diabetes, that can show up in the eyes. Questions about your work or studies and the ways you generally use your eyes will help to round out the picture.

The eye specialist uses a number of sophisticated instruments to examine the outer and inner parts of the eye. This examination may include the use of eye drops containing a drug such as phenylephrine, which dilates the pupil and permits better viewing of the eye's interior. There is some disagreement about the use of these drops, as well as other drugs that temporarily paralyze the focusing muscles of the eye so that the natural refraction of the cornea, lens, and other re-fracting media can be measured undistorted by the effects of the muscles. Many ophthalmologists and some optometrists use such drops as a standard part of the eye exam. But many optometrists argue strongly against them, claiming that a more accurate estimation of the eye's visual abilities can be obtained by observing the muscles and refracting media working together. (Remember, though, that in a number of states, optometrists are not allowed to administer eye medicines.) Vision should first be tested with the eye muscles working normally, before eye drops, if any, are used, since vision problems can result from muscle imbalances as well as refractive disorders.

At any rate, don't plan to read or drive or operate machinery after an eye exam; and it is a good idea to bring along a pair of sunglasses. If drops are used, you may be very sensitive to bright lights (because your pupils cannot adjust) and have difficulty focusing clearly for a few hours, until the effects of the drug wear off. Recently a major-league outfielder was sent to an ophthalmologist to have his eyes examined because he had been missing a lot of fly balls. His vision checked out perfectly, but then he had to miss that evening's game! His eyes took longer than usual to recover from the eye drops used in the exam, and he couldn't see well enough to play.

The instrument used to examine the interior of the eye is called an *ophthalmoscope*. This instrument lights up the interior of the eye and enlarges the image, so that the doctor can see the whole retina. Tiny arteries and veins can be seen crisscrossing the surface of the retina; in fact, this is the only place in the whole body where the blood vessels can be seen directly, and signs of diabetes, hardening of the arteries, or high blood pressure can be spotted. In addition, the doctor can detect any abnormalities of the retinal surface or of the optic nerve, which appears as a prominent light-colored round spot.

Diabetes, for example, can affect the eyes in various ways. There may be a blurring of vision that occurs and then clears up for no apparent reason; or a pair of glasses that was perfectly satisfactory may suddenly fail to provide clear vision, and an examination shows

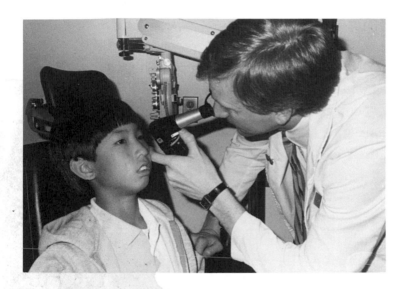

The modern eye doctor can use instruments such as the mon-
ocular indirect ophthalmoscope (top) and the binocular indirect
ophthalmoscope (bottom).

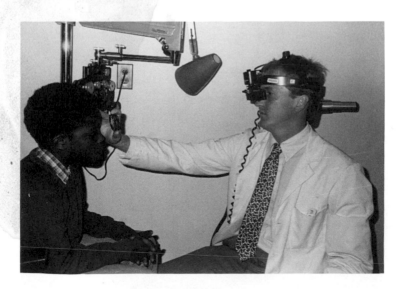

that a very different prescription for corrective lenses is now needed. These changes are due to a buildup of sugar in the blood and in the fluids inside the eye, which change the focus. (In fact, it is sometimes rather difficult to prescribe satisfactory glasses for diabetics, since the amount of sugar in the body fluids may fluctuate, continually changing the correction needed.) Diabetes may also temporarily weaken the muscles that move the eyes, producing double vision. Examination of the eye's interior can reveal early cataract, or iritis (an inflammation of the iris), both of which may be signs of diabetes. The disease also produces damaging changes in the blood vessels, which affect the tiny capillaries first. The eye specialist may see signs of tiny breaks and leakage of blood from the capillaries in the retina. If diabetes is not treated, by means of a special diet, insulin, or other measures to control the blood-sugar level, the changes in the retina may progress. Diabetes, in fact, is one of the leading causes of blindness.

A *slit-lamp microscope* gives the doctor a view of the front parts of the eye, including the cornea and lens. Focusing a bright light on the eye, it gives a detailed, three-dimensional view, magnified about ten to fifty times.

Variations of the *Snellen eye chart* are used to test the distance vision, first without glasses and later with an assembly of lenses made up to correspond to the new prescription. This eye chart was developed by a Dutch physician, Herman Snellen, in 1863. It is de-

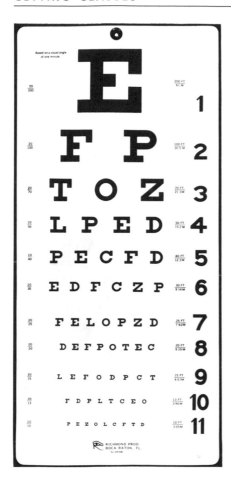

A reduced view of the Snellen eye chart.

signed to be viewed at 20 feet (about 6 meters), and the patient is asked to read off letters and numbers that get successively smaller with each line down. The vision score is expressed as a fraction determined by the last line you were able to read successfully. A score of 20/30, for example, means that you were able to read, from 20 feet away, a line that people with normal vision could make out at 30 feet. When the second number is larger, that means that your vision is not

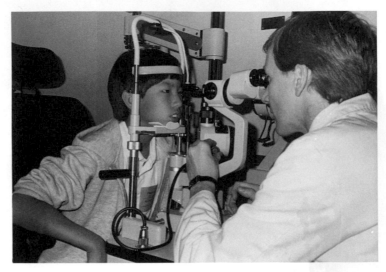

A slit-lamp microscope gives a magnified view of the cornea and lens.

as sharp as the norm. A score of 20/10, on the other hand, means that at 20 feet you can read letters that a person with normal vision would have to move up to 10 feet to see clearly. Since many rooms are not 20 feet long, the eye chart may be made correspondingly smaller so that the test can be run at a shorter distance. Another useful variation is to project lines of the chart on a screen. This permits the letters to be varied and may thus give a more accurate score. (Some people unconsciously memorize the standard eye chart and rattle the characters off from memory instead of reading them.) The vision of each eye is tested separately.

Other tests are used to determine nearsightedness, farsightedness, and astigmatism; to check eye coordination and eye muscle function to be sure the eyes are working together properly as a team; to test for depth perception, ability to judge distance, peripheral vision (the ability to detect shapes or movement at the edge of the field of vision), the ability to change focus easily from near to far and vice versa, or to adjust from light to darkness and back again; and to test color vision.

For people who are thirty-five or older, or who have family members with glaucoma, the eye test routinely includes a check for this disease. An instrument called a *tonometer* is used to determine the pressure inside the eyeball. Part of the device actually gently touches the surface of the cornea, but there is no danger nor any pain (not even any sensation at all, because the eye surface is numbed first with a drop of anesthetic).

Periodic examinations for glaucoma are very important. About 2 percent of all people over the age of thirty-five suffer from this condition. In the early stages—when prompt treatment can still prevent damage to vision—there may be no apparent symptoms. Normally, the fluid in the aqueous humor is constantly flowing, as new fluid is produced and the excess drains out. But if the drainage is poor, or if disease, injury, or some drug blocks off the drain openings, the pressure inside the eye builds up because new fluid is still flowing in and has nowhere to go. The pressure buildup may be very gradual; but eventually, if not detected and treated, it will damage the delicate fibers of the optic nerve. Then there will be

GLAUCOMA

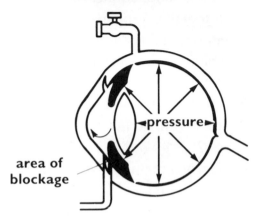

area of
blockage

NORMAL FLOW OF FLUID

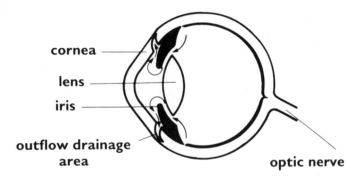

cornea

lens

iris

outflow drainage
area

optic nerve

*Fluid constantly flows through the aqueous humor of the eye. If
the drainage ducts are blocked, fluid accumulates inside the eyeball, and the pressure builds up. Eventually fibers of the optic
nerve can be damaged. This condition is called glaucoma.*

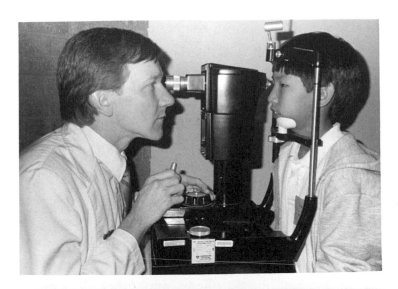

Instruments such as the noncontact tonometer shown at the top can be used to test for glaucoma, which may produce a "tunnel vision" distortion like that shown at the bottom.

blind spots in the vision; the peripheral vision may be lost entirely, producing a sort of "tunnel vision." Ultimately all vision may be lost: Glaucoma is one of the leading causes of blindness in the United States. Fortunately, early detection of the pressure buildup—in a routine eye exam before symptoms have developed—permits the use of special pressure-lowering medications (taken in the form of eye drops) or surgery to correct the drainage problem before any serious damage is done to the optic nerve.

An instrument called a *phoropter* is used for a number of tests of eye function. It consists of a frame on which various lenses, filters, and other devices are mounted. By flipping lenses and making other adjustments, literally billions of lens combinations can be tried out. Using this instrument, the eye doctor determines the refractive state of each eye: whether it is nearsighted, farsighted, astigmatic, or some combination. Part of the results are obtained by analyzing the movement of lights and shadows on the retina while the person stares into the distance and the light from an ophthalmoscope shines into the eye. Other information is provided by the patient's answers as the doctor tries various lens combinations, continually asking, "Is this better or worse? Clearer or less clear?"

A thorough vision examination should never be done quickly. All together, it may take thirty to sixty minutes. If you feel rushed or confused, don't hesitate to say so. If you don't understand a question, ask the doctor to repeat it and, if necessary, to explain.

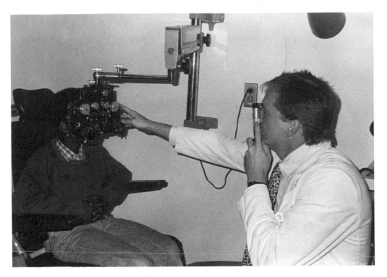

The phoropter or retinoscope is part of the modern eye examination. The doctor can examine the interior of the eye while trying various combinations of refracting lenses.

If a refractive disorder is found, the result of the eye examination will be a prescription for corrective lenses. Theoretically, using sophisticated instruments, any two eye doctors should come up with the same assessment of your eyes' refractive state. But their prescriptions might vary quite a bit, depending on how much of the disorder the lenses should correct. You might think that the ideal correction would supply whatever is needed to give you "perfect" 20/20 vision, both near and at a distance. In practice, however, it is often desirable not to correct all the way with lenses, leaving some of the work for the eye muscles to complete. The vision specialist's knowledge, experience, and judgment determine what the appropriate lens correction should be.

Reading the Prescription

A prescription for corrective lenses consists of numbers and symbols and may look very mysterious. Actually, with a few keys you can easily understand the simple code.

First of all, there are two sets of numbers, one for O.D. and one for O.S. These letters are abbreviations for Latin words. O.D. stands for *oculus dexter*, the right eye; O.S. is *oculus sinister*, the left eye. (Since the eyes probably differ, each one will need its own prescription.)

The correction to be built into the lens begins with a plus or minus, followed by a number, given to two decimal places: for example, +1.00, or −2.50. The plus (+) symbol indicates a convex lens (to converge light rays for a farsighted eye), and the minus (−) indicates a concave lens (to diverge light rays for a nearsighted eye). The number is the focusing power of the lens in diopters (or 1 divided by the focal length of the lens). One *diopter* (written as +1.00 D, or just +1.00) is the power needed to converge parallel light rays to a point 1 meter away. A +2.00 D lens would be twice as strong, focusing the same light rays to a point only half a meter away.

If the eye is also astigmatic, the prescription will have some more information, for example, $+1.25$ -0.75 axis 60. This is a lens for an eye with 1.25 diopters of farsightedness and 0.75 diopter of astigmatism. The axis, which can be any value from 1 to 180, indicates how the cylindrical portion of the lens should be oriented, based on the degrees of a protractor. The horizontal is 180; the vertical is 90. In other words, the finished lens will have an overall convex shape, but part of it will be ground to a precisely determined cylindrical shape. When the glasses are positioned properly in front of the eyes, the cylindrical portion compensates for the uneven curvature of the cornea, making it equivalent to the normal spherical curve, while the convex part of the lens provides the extra converging power needed to correct for the hyperopia.

An additional number, with a little triangular symbol (Δ), calls for the addition of a *prism*, a wedge-shaped lens, to change the direction of the light rays. The prism prescription will also specify the direction of the base of the prism: IN, OUT, UP, or DOWN.

The prescription may include corrections for both near and distance vision. For example,

$$+1.00 \; - \; 0.50 \text{ axis } 85$$
$$\text{add } +2.00$$

indicates that the person is farsighted, requiring 1 diopter of correction for distance. An additional 2 diopters (making a total of 3 diopters) of correction is needed for reading and close work. There is also a half-diopter correction for astigmatism. This prescription could be made up into two pairs of glasses, one for reading and the other for general use. Or one could get a single pair of bifocals, in which a small lens with the reading correction is built into a larger lens with the distance correction.

The prescription may also include the P.D. (*pupillary distance*). That is the distance in millimeters from the center of one pupil to the center of the other, measured with the person looking straight ahead. The corrective lenses will be ground so that their optical centers will exactly coincide with the centers of the pupils.

Sometimes the prescription specifies the *base curves*, the curvatures of the front and back of the lens. The combination of the two curves gives the lens its focusing power. Two lenses with quite different base curves may have exactly the same strength: For example, a lens with a front curve of $+6$ (convex) and a back curve of -4 (concave) would have the same power ($+6-4 = +2$) as a lens with front and back curves of $+1$ each ($+1+1 = +2$). Both lenses would provide the same correction for farsightedness, but the use of different combinations of base curves provides the eye specialist with an additional refinement that may be helpful in some cases. A person who switches to a new pair of glasses with a different base curve may feel uncomfortable for a few days (or even a few weeks). It is hard to adjust because the distance from the lens to the eye is not what the person is used to, and the distortions of the peripheral vision are different, too. Eventually, however, the person adapts to these changes, and the new curve becomes familiar.

Getting Glasses

Once the prescription for corrective lenses has been determined, you have some decisions to make. First of all, you need to decide whether to get eyeglasses or contact lenses. In the next chapter we'll discuss the pros and cons of contacts. Here let's talk about the various eyeglass options.

Choosing frames is an important part of getting a new pair of glasses. The optician will have a number of empty frames in a variety of shapes, sizes, and colors. By trying them on you can find the one that feels most comfortable and looks the best on you.

Should you pick plastic or metal frames? Thin gold or silver wire frames may be fashionable, but they do not hold their shape as well as plastic ones. If the frames bend or warp out of shape, you will not be looking out of the lenses at the correct angle, and the refractive correction will be slightly different. Then you may begin to feel uncomfortable or even suffer from eyestrain, particularly if you are astigmatic. A new type of wire frame, made from a space-age alloy that "remembers" its shape when heated, may be the best solution to that problem.

It's best to select a lens that is large enough so that you do not feel conscious of the frames. Oversize lenses, though, should generally be avoided, as there tends to be some distortion of the refraction near the edges. (When you look out through the middle of the lens, you are looking straight through it and seeing with exactly the prescribed correction. But when you turn your eyes and look out through an outer part of the lens, you are looking through it at an angle and getting a slightly different refraction.) Severely curved wraparound styles should be avoided for the same reason, even though they may seem like the height of fashion. If the glasses are to be used for reading only, you may want to consider small oval or half-moon-shaped glasses that permit you to look up over them to see something at a distance.

Which are better, glass or plastic lenses? Both are safe, for all eyeglass lenses are now required by law to be shatter resistant. Plastic lenses are usually lighter and therefore may be more comfortable than glass. They also have less tendency to fog. Disadvantages are that plastic lenses are more expensive, and they scratch more easily, so more care must be taken in cleaning them. (It is better to wash them with soap and water or detergent solution and blot dry with a soft cloth, rather than polish them. Lens paper designed for polishing glass lenses may scratch plastic.) A special chemical coating can be applied to polycarbonate plastic lenses to make them scratch resistant.

After you have chosen your frames, the optician will measure your pupillary distance (or remeasure it, if it is specified on the prescription). We had a first-hand experience of how important this measurement can be: One of us (the astigmatic one) got a new pair of glasses from an optometrist who had provided excellent prescriptions in the past. But reading, watching television, or driving with these new glasses seemed uncomfortable and soon produced severe eyestrain. Reexaminations by the optometrist generated some new ideas, such as inserting a prism, but that did not help. A visit to an ophthalmologist confirmed that the prescribed refractions were correct but revealed that the prescribed pupillary distance was about 3 millimeters too great, and the optical centers of the lenses were another 2 millimeters farther apart than that. (Although lenses are carefully checked by the eye doctor to make sure they correspond to the prescription, a little deviation is considered acceptable. Unfortunately, in this case both errors were in the same direction and added up to an unacceptable change.) A new pair of glasses, made by an independent optician according to the same prescription, provided clear, comfortable vision, and the eyestrain promptly disappeared.

If you need different corrections for near and distance vision, you must decide whether to get two pairs of glasses or one pair of bifocals. Choose the latter, and you have another set of options: How large should the reading lens be? And do you want bifocals in which there is an abrupt change in the prescription from one section to the next (so that a visible line marks the boundary) or a newer (and more expensive) variation in which the lens changes smoothly and gradually from one prescription to the other? This type of bifocal lens is often called "invisible," because there is no noticeable dividing line. Some people, though, find the distortions of the transition zone too confusing and uncomfortable and are unable to adjust to them. In either case, the transition from one prescription to the other should fall below the pupil of the eye when the wearer is looking straight ahead. Otherwise, the eyes are constantly trying to focus two different images at the same time and may become strained.

How large the reading lens in bifocals should be depends on how much reading you do, and what kinds. People who do a lot of reading or like to be able to scan a whole newspaper page will find a small reading

lens inconvenient. Some occupations have special re-
quirements. A druggist who needs to be able to read
labels on high shelves and an electrician doing over-
head wiring can both use bifocals with two reading
segments, one at the top and the other at the bottom
of the lens. A violinist who plays in an orchestra may
need trifocals: one segment for looking at the con-
ductor, a stronger magnification for reading music on
the stand, and a still stronger correction for ordinary
reading at a closer distance.

The preparation of the lenses includes hundreds of
grindings and painstaking tests for accuracy. In the
final step, the optician fits the glasses and may bend
or adjust the frames, tailoring them to your individual
needs so that they fit comfortably and rest securely,
with the lenses evenly aligned.

If you are buying over-the-counter glasses, you will
not get this kind of individual fitting. There are some
precautions you can take, though, to get a pair of
glasses that will suit your needs. First of all, check to
make sure the lenses are mounted securely, with their
edges fitting evenly into the grooves in the frame. Otherwise, a blow to the face might pop them out into
your eyes. Check the lenses for flaws: They are mass
produced, and small irregularities could distort or blur
your vision. You can pick up such imperfections by
looking at a horizontal line with the glasses on, then
turning your head to view the line from different an-
gles. If the line seems to ripple, look for another pair
of glasses. Also check the fit of the frame carefully. If

it is uncomfortable now, it will feel even worse after long wearing; and a lopsided fit or a tendency to slip down your nose could result in eyestrain.

Getting Used to Glasses

A new pair of eyeglasses requires some adjustments, especially if it is your first pair.

One psychological hurdle is the idea of having to wear glasses. The diagnosis of a refractive disorder may feel like a kind of defeat—failing a test—and the corrective glasses are tangible evidence that you do not have perfect vision. Well, nobody's perfect, and if one of your imperfections is your vision, you have plenty of company—about half the population.

Still, it is rather a jolt to realize you have to wear glasses if you want to see clearly, especially if this is a recent problem and you've enjoyed excellent vision before. Getting used to wearing glasses may also be difficult for young children, who do not fully understand the reason for them, or who may be teased by friends or schoolmates. It can be even harder for teenagers, who are going through a number of confusing and upsetting changes and don't need another problem. They may worry that wearing glasses will make them unattractive. But with all of today's fashionable eyewear styles, and rock stars and other celebrities sporting the latest "shades," the time when "Men seldom make passes/At girls who wear glasses" is long gone! These days, eyeglasses can be fashion accessories even for people who don't need them. A recent survey of recruiters for large corporations revealed that people wearing glasses make a positive impression: intelligent, professional, businesslike.

There are some physical adjustments to new glasses too. Your brain has gotten used to interpreting visual messages in a certain way, on the basis of your own faulty vision or your last pair of glasses. The new glasses may eventually make things much clearer, but at first things may seem tilted, out of focus, or just uncomfortably wrong. Getting used to bifocals for the first time is even harder, since the eyes and brain must learn to switch rapidly back and forth between the two prescriptions. Don't get discouraged or immediately demand a new prescription. Give it a try for a few days, or even a few weeks before you consider going back for a reexamination. Eventually you will probably adjust and discover that you are seeing better than ever before.

6

CONTACT LENS OPTIONS

IF YOU HAVE EVER HAD a speck in your eye, you probably recall vividly how irritating it was. A tiny particle, barely big enough to see, bothered you constantly until it was removed—or perhaps even a while longer. How, then, could anyone possibly tolerate something as large as a contact lens?

Oddly enough, although the eye is acutely sensitive to small foreign bodies, it is rather insensitive to larger objects that follow the contour of the eyeball. If it were not, the contact with your own eyelids would soon drive you crazy! Properly fitted contact lenses should not feel any less comfortable than your own eyelids. (Hard contact lenses take some adjusting to before they feel comfortable, since the edges of the

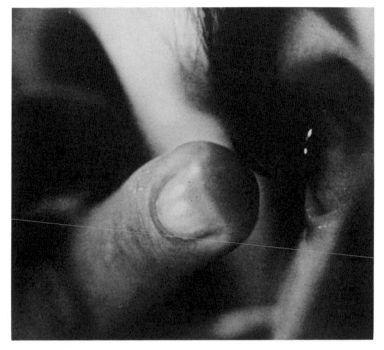

A hard contact lens.

lens are felt by the inside of the eyelid with each blink; with soft contact lenses, this rubbing effect does not occur.)

How Contact Lenses Work

A contact lens is a very thin plastic lens that is worn on the front surface of the eye. The lens rests on the cornea, separated from its actual surface by a thin film of tears. You may have noticed while washing dishes that if two wet plates are stacked together, they resist your efforts to pull them apart, although you may be able to slide one surface along the other. The tension of the film of water between them is what holds them together. The contact lens stays in place according to the same principle of surface tension. At each blink it slides slightly over the surface of the cornea, but it does not come off.

The first practical contact lenses for general use were the *hard lenses*, made of a transparent plastic called polymethyl methacrylate (PMMA). This substance can provide a clear, sharp refractive correction, but it does not permit any oxygen to pass through. The cornea, remember, does not have its own blood-vessel supply. It must get its nourishment mainly from the air and tears. If the hard contact lens stayed firmly in place all the time, the cornea would not be able to "breathe," and it would soon be damaged. Hard contact lenses are designed to move slightly with each blink of the eye, creating a pumping action that draws in fresh, oxygen-rich tears and flushes out the stale ones from under the lens. That is enough to keep the cells of the cornea going for a while, but they do not get as much oxygen as they would without the lens. That is why wearers of hard contact lenses must remove them each night and sleep without them. First-time wearers need a long time to get used to hard lenses; it may take up to four weeks before they feel comfortable.

In recent years, new materials have been developed for use in hard contact lenses to allow oxygen and other gases to pass through them. These *gas-permeable lenses* allow more oxygen to reach the cornea and are more comfortable to wear for longer periods of time. One type, made of a combination of PMMA and silicone, can produce just as good a vision correction as the standard hard lenses. Another type, made of cellulose acetate butyrate (CAB), may give wearers some fluctuations of vision. The Boston Equalens, introduced in 1987, is made from a Teflon-like nonstick fluoropolymer material that is naturally resistant to the buildup of protein deposits, which often cause eye irritations with other types of lenses. All these gas-permeable lenses need less adaptation time than hard lenses, about seven to ten days.

Soft lenses, introduced in the 1970s and 1980s, are made of various flexible, water-absorbing plastics. After they absorb water they become soft and gas permeable and are much more comfortable. Typically, they require only three to seven days of adaptation for first-time wearers, and they can be worn on and off without any need for readapting to them. They are much less likely than hard lenses to pop out during action sports, and there is very little chance of dust or dirt getting under a soft lens and irritating the eye. (This can be a problem with hard lenses.) But soft lenses may not provide as good a vision correction; they are harder to clean, less durable than hard lenses, and need replacement after a year or less.

Some soft lenses are removed and cleaned each day, like the hard lenses. But *extended-wear soft lenses*, available since 1979, are so permeable to oxygen that they can be worn continuously for periods of up to thirty days. Usually it is better to remove and clean them more often, because they tend to accumulate deposits that can irritate the eyes or even produce painful ulceration of the cornea. The buildup of deposits also shortens the lifetime of the lenses to six

A soft contact lens.

months or less. Most eye specialists believe that except under special circumstances the extra convenience of extended-wear soft lenses is not enough to compensate for their drawbacks and dangers.

In 1987 *disposable soft lenses* were introduced. These plastic contact lenses are meant to be worn around the clock for a week and then thrown away. They can solve the problems of eye irritation and possible damage caused by extended-wear soft lenses, but *only* if they are used properly. Some eye specialists are afraid that people may try to save money by wearing the disposable lenses longer than they are supposed to. (The cost of disposable lenses is estimated at about $520 a year, compared to about $350 a year for extended-wear soft lenses and the special solutions used to clean them.)

Both hard and soft lenses can correct all the main kinds of refractive disorders: myopia, hyperopia, presbyopia, and astigmatism. (Those designed for astigmatism are called *toric* lenses. Effectively they form a new front surface for the eye, compensating for the irregularities of the cornea.)

Bifocal contact lenses are available in both hard and soft forms but generally are more difficult to fit than the single-prescription lenses. The slight shifts in position as the lenses ride on the tear film that coats the cornea can be disconcerting and make them less effective than bifocal eyeglasses. There are several interesting options in design. One type is similar to bifocal glasses, with the reading portion at the bottom; in hard lens versions the lens is weighted at the bottom to keep it from rotating the reading portion out of position, whereas soft lenses have less of a tendency to shift position. Soft lenses can be made with a central zone for distance and the outer zone for reading (or vice versa), which allows the wearer to read comfortably in any position. Some people, however, have annoying "ghost" images with this type of lens.

People with presbyopia may be able to achieve good vision at all distances by wearing a contact lens with a distance correction on one eye and a contact lens for near vision on the other eye. The brain learns to switch automatically from one eye's focus to the other, depending on whether a close or distant object is being viewed. This approach is called *monovision*. Still another alternative is to wear contact lenses that correct for distance vision and use a pair of reading glasses with them for close work.

In 1988 the British optical firm Pilkington announced an entirely new approach to bifocal contact lenses. The design grew out of research on displays for fighter pilots. It is based on the principle of *holography*, which is also the basis of the brightly colored pictures on credit cards and novelty items that show one view when looked at straight on and switch to a different position (or a different picture altogether) when seen at an angle. In the holographic contact lens, the shape of the lens compensates in the normal way for the wearer's main vision defect and focuses the image of distant objects sharply onto the retina. The prescription for close vision is incorporated into a diffraction grating on the inner part of the lens. (A diffraction grating is an array of narrowly spaced lines that bends light rays so that they form a pattern of dark and light bands.) This device refracts some of the light rays from close objects so that the focus falls in front of the retina. When the person is looking at a distant object, the close image does not register on the retina; no messages about the object are sent to the brain, and it is not "seen." But when the person looks at a close object, the action of eye muscles brings the image from the diffraction grating into sharp focus on the retina, while the image of distant objects moves out of focus and is ignored by the brain's visual centers. This new lens can provide a much more natural type of vision than other bifocal designs, since the entire lens is used for viewing both close and distant objects.

Still another contact lens option is the tinted lens, available in both hard and soft forms. Some tinted contact lenses actually change the apparent color of a person's eyes. So if you always thought you'd look better with blue eyes instead of your natural brown, you can improve on nature with contact lenses.

Contact Lens Wear and Care

You may have seen ads for contact lenses that can be purchased by mail order. They are not a good idea.

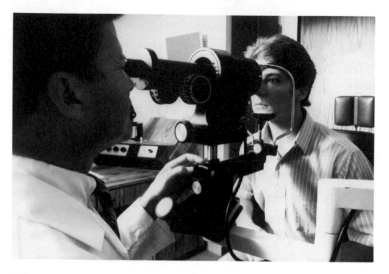

A keratometer measures the curvature of the cornea.

Fitting contact lenses is a task for an expert. The eye doctor uses an instrument called a *keratometer* to measure the curvature of your cornea. The entire surface of the cornea must be carefully mapped, for each eye is unique, and the contact lens must be precisely designed for it. The lens must fit tightly enough to stay on without slipping around or rubbing, but loosely enough to permit an exchange of tears to nourish the cornea. When the contact lens is made to the doctor's measurements, the refractive corrections are incorporated, just as they are in the grinding of eyeglass lenses.

The fitting process includes complete, hands-on instructions on how to insert and remove your new contact lenses. Try not to feel nervous or rushed. If

you have questions, ask them; and practice inserting
and removing the lenses in the presence of the doctor
or assistant until you are confident about the techniques. If you feel you need another practice session,
go back for it—most reputable lens fitters provide all
the follow-up help you need without any extra charge.
If you have trouble putting in the contacts by yourself
when you get home, don't wear them until you have
gotten some more instructions.

During the adjustment period, your eyes may tear,
and the lens may slide out of place. Don't panic. Just
look in a mirror—a magnifying-type makeup mirror
is best—and slide it back into place. You don't have
to worry about it sliding behind your eyeball and
getting lost—that can't happen. And an out-of-place
lens won't cause any harm to the eye, so you don't
need to hurry to get it back into place.

If some irritation occurs during the first week or
two, *don't* rub your eyes. If the irritation doesn't gradually ease, or your eyes burn, are painful, are sensitive
to light, or are very red, or if you begin to see "rain-
bows" around lights, take out the lenses and talk to
your doctor.

As you adjust to the contact lenses, you can gradually increase the time you wear them each day, up
to the limit your doctor recommends. Don't go beyond
the limit. If you want to wear your lenses during the
day and then need them for a late-night party, you
may be tempted to cheat "just this once." If you do,
you may pay for it in an irritation that forces you to

stop wearing the lenses for a day or two. Instead, just take out the lenses for an hour before the party, and then you can wear them for another six or eight hours.

If you insert and remove contact lenses over a sink, be sure to put the stopper in or cover the drain with a towel. Otherwise, if you drop a lens, you may find yourself looking for a wrench to open up the drainpipes. A better idea is to remove and insert lenses over a table, and use a plastic squeeze bottle with water or rinsing liquid and a small glass to clean the lenses.

No matter how careful you are, you will probably drop the lenses sometimes. Then comes a frantic hunt—and you don't have the clear vision that your lenses provide. When you do find a dropped hard lens, wet the tip of a finger, touching it to the lens, and lift the

Inserting a contact lens.

lens straight up. Don't slide the lens along a surface; you may scratch it. You can pick up a dropped soft lens by sliding a piece of paper under it. While you were looking for the lens, it was drying out, and it may become brittle and easily damaged. Place the lens in its solution to restore its flexible state. (A dropped hard contact lens should also be put into its solution before it is reinserted into the eye.)

Be sure to put your lenses in the right compartments when you put them into their case. Unless you pay attention, you may accidentally switch the right and left lenses. If their prescriptions are not the same, the world will look pretty strange when you put the lenses in again.

The most important part of caring for contact lenses—the hard and especially the soft ones—is to clean and sterilize them regularly, *using the method your doctor recommends*. Don't try to save money by using a homemade cleaner instead of the commercial sterilizing solution.

A recent telephone survey of five hundred contact lens wearers, sponsored by the Food and Drug Administration, revealed that quite a few of them had some wrong (and potentially dangerous) ideas about how to care for their lenses. Nearly a third believed that saline (salt) or cleaning solution disinfected the lenses. (In fact, such solutions can actually become breeding grounds for germs.) Some people thought they could use dishwashing liquid to disinfect their lenses. Among those using daily-wear lenses, 11 percent did not know they were supposed to take the lenses out each day to clean and sterilize them.

Such wrong ideas can cause a lot of harm. Failing to clean and disinfect contact lenses correctly and often enough allows harmful bacteria and other microorganisms to grow and multiply. In the mid-1980s, eye specialists were alarmed to note a steep increase in cases of a rare kind of corneal infection, caused by an amoeba normally found in water and soil. This microbe, *Acanthamoeba*, feeds on yeast cells and bacteria and does not cause any trouble in its natural home. But in the eye, sheltered in the tear film under a contact lens, it produces a raging inflammation of the cornea. None of the available drugs are very effective against this microbe. In some cases, acanthamoeba keratitis leads to loss of vision in the infected eye or even to loss of the eyeball. Although this problem is very rare (less than one hundred cases were reported from 1973 to mid-1987, compared with the millions of contact lens wearers), most of the cases have occurred since 1985. A study conducted by the Centers for Disease Control revealed that the patients, mainly wearers of soft contact lenses, were more likely than a comparison group of healthy wearers to have used homemade saline solutions and to have disinfected their lenses less often than the manufacturers recommend.

Regular eye examinations, every six months, can help to make sure that your lenses are in good condition and your eyes are healthy. Wearing hard lenses, in particular, makes the eyes less sensitive to pain, and you may not realize they are being damaged by a dirty or contaminated lens.

Pros and Cons of Contact Lenses

There are difficulties in adjusting to contact lenses. Dexterity is needed to insert and remove them. And there are risks of damage to the eyes if you are not conscientious enough in following the doctor's recommendations for their wearing and cleaning. So why would people choose this form of vision correction instead of the traditional eyeglasses? There are a number of good reasons.

Most people who wear contact lenses chose them for the sake of appearance. They feel that they would not look as attractive in eyeglasses. It is no coincidence that there are more female contact lens wearers than male; in general, women tend to be more concerned about their appearance than men. Models and actors may choose contact lenses to avoid distracting reflections from the lights that give people with eyeglasses an "owl-eyed" look in front of the camera. During his presidency, Ronald Reagan, who is nearsighted but also suffers from presbyopia, sometimes wore just one contact lens when he was making a speech. He could see the audience with his corrected eye and glance down at the text of his speech with the other.

There are some other good reasons for wearing contact lenses instead of eyeglasses. Contact lenses can provide better and more natural vision. With glasses, only the very center of each lens is perfectly focused; when you look off at an angle, there is some distortion, and the frames interfere with peripheral vision. But a contact lens is very thin, very close to the eye, and it moves with the eye. The center of the lens always stays lined up perfectly in front of the pupil, so the lens is always in perfect focus. Peripheral vision is good in every direction, and there are no bulky frames to block it. In addition, contact lenses don't fog up in cold weather or get spattered with raindrops. The eyelids, which act like natural windshield wipers for the eyes, keep contact lenses clear too.

Contact lenses are safe to wear for sports, and they are more convenient than eyeglasses, which might slip, fog up, or fall off at a crucial moment. (An exception is swimming: Although contact lenses are safe, they may float away and get lost.)

In cases where the cornea is scarred, irregularly shaped, or cone shaped, contact lenses may be the only way to achieve good vision. The tiny lens, exactly fitted to the contours of the cornea, smooths out its irregularities and focuses images just as though the cornea were perfectly curved. In certain diseases, or after burns of the eye, contact lenses can also promote healing of the cornea.

Contact lenses do have their disadvantages, though. They are harder to put on and take off than glasses, and they are more trouble to clean. It may be a temptation to leave them in longer than you are supposed to, or to be a little sloppy about cleaning them. Mistakes like those can be very costly. Dirty contact lenses can damage the corneas and may promote infections; they can even result in blindness!

For anyone who needs glasses only for certain activities, such as reading or driving, contact lenses are more of a nuisance than they are worth. (There are an estimated fourteen million occasional and former contact lens wearers who do not use the lenses regularly because of inconvenience or eye irritation.) But many full-time wearers find the routine of contact lens use and care well worth the trouble, especially if their vision disorders would require very heavy, thick-lensed eyeglasses.

An important disadvantage of contact lenses is their cost. In general, contact lenses cost considerably more than eyeglasses, and they may need replacement more often. Commercial cleaning solutions required for proper lens care add to the cost of wearing contacts.

Some people simply cannot tolerate contact lenses, even after a reasonable period of adaptation. Often these people react strongly to eye drops placed in the eyes. Others may find that their eyes become sensitive and readily irritated after they have been using contact lenses for some time. Ophthalmologists have discovered that these people have developed an allergy to tiny airborne particles that collect on the surface of the lenses. Such particles include common allergens like ragweed pollen, house dust, and dust mites (microscopic insects that thrive in carpets and other house furnishings). In sensitive people these allergens cause a sandpapery feeling when the lenses are in place, blurred vision, gooey mucus discharges, and redness of the eyes. The inner surface of the eyelid becomes red and bumpy. People who develop this kind of allergy may be able to continue wearing contact lenses under a doctor's supervision if they are very careful about cleaning the lenses and limit their wearing time.

People whose eyes do not produce enough tears cannot wear contact lenses successfully. Conditions such as pregnancy and diabetes can lead to dry eyes. Certain medications, including birth control pills, antihistamines, and decongestants, can also cut down tear production.

If you are one of the majority who can tolerate contact lenses, should you wear them? Do the advantages outweigh the nuisances and risks? That is a decision only you can make.

7

TODAY'S OPTIONS FOR SPECIAL NEEDS

RESEARCHERS at the University of Rochester recently announced that "sunglasses" for the camera lens screened out confusing data and made their robots' vision systems much more effective. Rose-tinted contact lenses are calming down chickens caged on modern farms and keeping them from fighting. Soft contact lenses are used to hold medications in place in the eyes of horses. And a pair of custom-made contact lens sunglasses was designed to relieve the discomfort of a deep-water shark in the brightly lit waters of a San Francisco aquarium.

Applications like these may seem a bit farfetched, but lenses for special needs are also helping people all over the world.

Special Lenses for Special Needs

Each year thousands of children and adults suffer serious eye injuries in sports such as racquetball, hockey, and soccer. In addition to flying projectiles (a hard racquetball can reach speeds of up to 130 miles per hour), hockey sticks, baseball bats, and even the fingers or knees of opponents can cause severe damage if they come in contact with an eye. Many of these injuries could be avoided by wearing safety glasses.

All eyeglasses are shatter resistant in normal use, but they may not provide enough protection for sports. New York Mets outfielder Mookie Wilson found that out the hard way during spring training in 1986, when he was accidentally hit by a ball in a practice session. His eyeglass lens shattered, and his eyeball was cut. Fortunately he recovered without any loss of vision, but he missed part of his team's World Championship season.

Eye specialists recommend that safety eyewear should be worn for sports such as rifle shooting, motorcycling, skiing, and tobogganing, as well as hockey, racquetball, and baseball—even by people who do not wear corrective lenses. (If you need a refractive correction, safety goggles can be worn over your regular glasses, or the prescription can be made up in safety glasses.) The lenses of these special protective glasses should be made of *polycarbonate*, an especially strong, tough plastic, and they should be set in safety frames with a sturdy, shock-absorbing construction and extra deep grooves to hold the lenses securely.

Safety goggles can also cut down the accident toll in occupations like welding, painting, or carpentry, as well as potentially dangerous activities like mowing the family lawn. (Small pebbles thrown up by the mower blades can fly up into an eye.)

Specially tinted glasses can help color-blind people to distinguish colors—for example, the red and green that look similar to people with one common type of color blindness. A red-tinted contact lens developed in the late 1960s may be of aid. It is worn on the nondominant eye and helps to make colors more distinguishable by increasing the contrast between red and green. Tinted lenses for the color-blind cause problems in depth perception, though, and thus may not be suitable for routine use.

Binoculars with sophisticated electronic circuitry that amplifies the available light can help people to see in near darkness. Originally developed for the U.S. Army for use in night patrols, these vision aids are now helping people with *retinitis pigmentosa*, a disease in which an early symptom is night blindness.

A number of other vision aids are helping to bring sight to people with *low vision*, usually in the range of visual acuity from 20/70 to 20/200. These include telescopic lenses that fasten onto ordinary spectacles for distance vision, microscopic lenses for reading and close work, hand-held or mounted magnifiers, and special reading lenses for reading regular print. People with low vision can also benefit from special large-

A telescopic lens can aid a person with low vision.

print editions of books and magazines such as *Reader's Digest*, "talking books" from the Library of Congress, and playing cards with enlarged numbers and symbols. At Overbrook School for the Blind in Philadelphia, children with low vision can enjoy a fairyland of bright colors in a special "rainbow" room, decorated with glowing fluorescent paintings, toys, and educational aids lit by ultraviolet light. This is a harmless kind of ultraviolet, filtered through black light bulbs, and it can increase color perception by as much as 600 percent in comparison with ordinary light. People with low vision used to be advised to "save" their eyesight by using it as little as possible. But now vision aids permit them to utilize what visual acuity they have to live a fuller, more satisfying life.

A more frivolous use of special lenses is the filter glasses used by audiences at 3-D movies to get three-dimensional illusions of depth. Some of the glasses have one red and one green lens, others neutral-colored filter lenses, depending on the kind of process used to make the film. Some people who try to watch 3-D movies with the special glasses see double or develop an eyestrain headache. This may be a sign of faulty eye coordination. The American Optometric Association recommends that people who have trouble with 3-D glasses should have their vision checked by a specialist. Eye coordination problems can interfere with driving, sports, or other activities that require good depth perception, but they can be corrected by prescription lenses or special eye exercises.

Do You Need Sunglasses?

Many eye specialists have a surprising answer to that question: Probably not. The eye, they point out, has its own built-in systems for adjusting to bright lights. In addition to the automatic constriction of the pupil, bright light stimulates chemical reactions in the rod and cone cells of the retina, decreasing their sensitivity to light. When the amount of light decreases, these chemical reactions reverse, and the sensitivity of the retina increases. These chemical adjustments are referred to as *adaptation*, and they take a little time. Have you noticed how dark the room looks when you first come inside on a bright sunny day? Soon things look normal again. After a while in a dark room, you may begin to make out the outlines of things, even though it seemed at first that there was no light at all. Because of these natural systems, some experts say, wearing dark glasses is unnecessary except under special conditions.

Fliers, skiers, and others who must cope with bright light and high glare find tinted lenses helpful in keeping vision comfortable and strain free. Our son, a computer scientist, has discovered that lightly tinted glasses cut the glare from his computer screen and help to keep him from developing a headache during a long work session. And a daughter, a nursing student, has found that tinted lenses cut the glare of the fluorescent lighting at the hospital.

Glasses with dark-gray glass lenses effectively screen out glare in bright sunlight and permit the wearer to see colors almost normally. Green or brown lenses provide protection from glare but distort colors. Yellow lenses can increase visibility on a cloudy day for hunters, pilots, or tennis players, but are not as good for sunny days. Pink lenses may make the world look rosy, but they do not screen out glare very well. The tinted lenses worn as a fashion accessory are generally too light to provide effective sun protection.

Glare from the screen or a poor work setup can lead to eyestrain in workers with computer terminals.

Actually, many sunglasses (especially the cheap ones) do not provide good protection from the most harmful of the sun's rays: the ultraviolet (the rays that cause sunburn; if strong enough, they can blister the cornea) and the infrared (heat rays, which can burn the retina). Cheap sunglasses can actually be dangerous, since their tint may make you think they are protecting your eyes when actually they are not. You should never, by the way, look directly at the sun, even if you are wearing sunglasses. A good grade of glass lens can filter out both ultraviolet and infrared rays effectively, but most sunglasses with plastic lenses do not filter out infrared rays, which are a problem mainly in hot climates. *Polaroid* sunglass lenses, first put on the market in the 1930s, selectively block light rays of certain vibrations and are effective in eliminating glare.

Photochromic glass darkens to a smoky gray when it is exposed to light; the brighter the light, the darker the glass becomes. It thus can act as an "automatic sunglass," providing protection from glare when a person goes out on a sunny day and then lightening after a return indoors. The wearer can thus avoid the inconvenience of having to carry an extra pair of glasses and change them continually. A friend of ours who lives in Florida says she can't imagine choosing anything else. But in less sunny climates, photochromic sunglasses may be merely an expensive nuisance. It takes some time for the lenses to lighten after coming indoors, so that the room seems dark; and the lenses tend gradually to darken, reducing the amount of light available to the eyes. This difference can be especially important for older people, since studies show that the amount of light needed for comfortable reading increases greatly with age.

A new sunglass option, the "Rollens," may make sun protection more convenient. The lightweight frameless plastic lenses come coiled like a roll of film and can be carried in a shirt pocket. When unrolled, they fit over the bridge of the nose and stay in place with a slight tension at the temples. Providing protection against both ultraviolet and infrared rays, these sunshades can be worn under regular glasses.

Replacing Nature's Lenses

Perhaps the most exciting uses of special lenses are the new surgical techniques that are literally bringing sight to the blind. A *cataract* is a clouding of the lens of the eye, which decreases its transparency and eventually makes it white and opaque. Light rays cannot reach the retina, and the person becomes blind. Some people are born with cataracts, which may cover all or only a small portion of the lens, but more often a cataract is a condition of older people. Sight can be restored by surgically removing the clouded lens and then compensating for its refracting power with special eyeglasses or contact lenses. In 1949 the first *intraocular lens* was implanted to replace an opaque lens. The plastic lens material, Perspex, was developed after a British ophthalmologist noticed that World War II fighter pilots injured by fragments of shattered airplane windows seemed able to tolerate bits of the plastic lodged in their eyes. Surgeons refined the lens implanting techniques in the 1970s and 1980s, and now the operation is commonplace. The implant can be put in when the clouded lens is removed, or it can be done years later. The artificial lens gives the cataract patient a much more attractive appearance than thick-lensed cataract glasses, while providing much more normal vision. (It cannot change focus like the natural lens, but it provides a similar field of vision. Cataract glasses, in contrast, usually give rather poor peripheral vision.) The intraocular lens also eliminates the difficulties people with poor sight have in removing and caring for contact lenses.

Living Lenses

For people with cataracts, hard-to-treat nearsightedness, and eye injuries, "living contact lenses" are providing a new hope of normal vision. The material for these "lenses" is donated corneas from people who have died. Because of its unique lack of a direct blood supply, the cornea is not as likely as other body tissues to be rejected if it is transplanted from one person to another. A transplanted kidney, for example, will be attacked by the immune system of the person who received it unless it comes from an identical twin or special drugs are used to temporarily knock out the immune defenses. With a cornea, such extreme precautions are not necessary.

The corneal transplant, in which a cloudy or damaged cornea is replaced, has been a routine surgical approach to restoring lost vision for decades. A newer surgical technique called *epikeratophakia* is now being used to correct faulty vision. In this operation, a piece of a donated cornea is freeze-dried, ground up, and shaped to the correct prescription for a contact lens to correct the vision. Then this custom-fitted "lens" is sewn onto the front of the eye. In time, cells from the patient's own cornea grow into the transplanted tissue, and it becomes a living part of the eye. The cornea is thus reshaped to provide a great improvement of vision.

"Braces" for the Eyes

Some eye specialists are using hard contact lenses to correct nearsightedness—not just temporarily, while the lenses are in, but permanently, so that eventually the person will no longer need corrective lenses. This technique, called *orthokeratology*, is still very controversial. It aims to compensate for the elongated shape of the myopic eyeball by flattening the cornea. This is done very gradually, by carefully measuring the curvature of the cornea and then fitting a hard contact lens that produces a slight flattening. After a while, a new lens is used to flatten it a little more, and so on, until 20/20 vision has been achieved. Orthokeratology is thus rather similar to orthodontics, a technique of dentistry in which poorly aligned teeth are slowly and gradually moved into better positions by the forces exerted by braces.

When satisfactory vision has been obtained without any more need for correction, the contact lens wearing time is gradually reduced. Some people find that their myopia has been cured, but for most the reshaped cornea begins to creep back toward its original curve. Then "retainer" lenses are fitted to hold the shape of the cornea. Depending on how the eyes respond, these lenses must be worn eight hours a day for some or as little as a few hours every month or two for others.

Eye specialists do not agree on how valuable orthokeratology is for achieving permanent vision correction. Many believe that the potential drawbacks outweigh the benefits; permanent distortion of the cornea can arise, sometimes as a delayed effect years after the treatment.

Reshaping Eyes

The majority of eye specialists tend to look with disfavor on another, even more controversial, technique for curing myopia: *radial keratotomy.* "Tomy" comes from a Greek word meaning "to cut," and in this procedure tiny cuts like the spokes of a wheel are made in the corneal surface. Scars are created as the cuts heal and cause the cornea to change its shape, flattening to decrease the nearsightedness. The amount of the change cannot always be predicted, and specialists are not yet sure what the long-term results of such surgery may be.

More precisely predictable results can be obtained by a newer form of corneal surgery: *keratomileusis,* or corneal carving. The surgeon slices away a portion of the outer part of the cornea, freezes it, and delicately reshapes the underside. For nearsightedness, part of the center portion is pared away to flatten the cornea; for farsightedness, the outer edges are sliced away, producing a greater curvature. The reshaped section

A. RADIAL KERATOTOMY

B. KERATOMILEUSIS

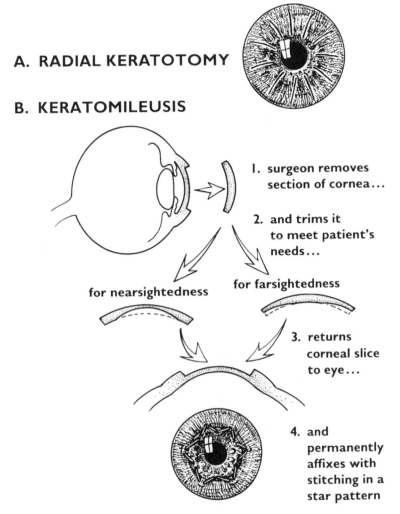

1. surgeon removes section of cornea...

2. and trims it to meet patient's needs...

for nearsightedness

for farsightedness

3. returns corneal slice to eye...

4. and permanently affixes with stitching in a star pattern

New surgical techniques are designed to produce permanent corrections of vision problems. In radial keratotomy, tiny cuts on the cornea, placed like the spokes on a wheel, permit a flattening of the curvature that may correct myopia. In keratomileusis, the surgeon custom carves a section of the cornea to correct refraction problems.

is then reattached to the eyeball, stitched on in a star-shaped pattern.

Some more recent advances may ultimately make other types of corneal surgery obsolete and provide realistic new options for people who cannot (or do not want to) wear glasses or contact lenses.

One new technique, announced in 1987 by researchers at Louisiana State University (LSU) Eye Center, uses an *excimer laser*, a finely focused beam of high-energy light, for corneal sculpting. With the aid of a computer, the surgeon reshapes the cornea precisely to correct for myopia, hyperopia, or astigmatism. (The technique can also replace epikeratophakia.) The laser surgery can be done without anesthesia and without the need for a hospital stay; the procedure takes only ten seconds! It is also designed to be as foolproof as possible: If the patient sneezes, for example, the laser automatically turns off, a video image of the eye just before the sneeze is retained, and the surgery picks up again when the patient is settled. In other types of cornea reshaping, the results depend on how well the eye heals. But according to LSU ophthalmologist Marguerite McDonald, the computer-controlled laser surgery, now being tested, may have much more consistent and predictable results.

Another bold new surgical technique for correcting faulty eyes uses *intrastromal corneal rings*. A small plastic ring, about 7 millimeters in diameter, is implanted in the cornea to change its curvature and optical properties and thus correct vision defects. If a person's vision needs later change, the ring can be removed and replaced by a new one with a suitably modified shape. Developed by Keravision, a Santa Clara, California, firm, this technique is now undergoing clinical testing. Although these new surgical techniques can literally reshape eyes for perfect vision, LSU researcher Marguerite McDonald believes that most people who can wear glasses or contact lenses probably will still choose to do so. "Anyone would have to agree," she cautions, "that glasses or contacts, if you can wear them, are preferable to any surgery."

8

EYE
EXERCISES
AND
EYE CARE

IN THE EARLY 1900s a New York City ophthalmologist, William H. Bates, started a revolution (or perhaps we should say counterrevolution) in his medical
specialty. From observations of his patients, his per-
sonal experiences, and forty years of research, Dr.
Bates became convinced that for many people with
vision defects, eyeglasses are not only unnecessary but
even harmful. Wearing glasses, he claimed, gradually
worsens the vision, so that stronger and stronger prescriptions are needed. His experiments with animals
suggested that the lens and ciliary muscles are not the
only factors in accommodation (or perhaps not even
the major factors). He discovered that the external
muscles that move the eyeball can alter its shape, thus

changing the eye's focus. He devised a series of eye exercises that became known as the Bates Method and wrote a best-selling book describing techniques to enable people to see better without glasses.

The medical establishment was skeptical (the American Medical Association dropped Dr. Bates from its membership rolls in 1912), and the techniques he recommended remain extremely controversial. Most eye specialists today believe that eye exercises can be useful in treating certain eye disorders, in particular those due to muscle imbalance. But they think that refractive disorders are generally determined by the physical nature of the eye and cannot be helped to any great degree by exercises. Still, devoted Bates disciples continue to practice and write books describing their techniques and successes.

Some of the Bates exercises are aimed at helping the eye muscles and the body as a whole to relax. Simply resting the eyes from time to time during reading or close work—closing them or looking off into the distance to change focus—can help to avoid eyestrain. In palming, you close your eyes and cover them with the palms of your hands, blocking out all light. Meanwhile, you try to visualize the blackest black you can imagine. Swinging is another relaxation exercise, which is also recommended as a bedtime prelude to more restful sleep: Turning the body rhythmically from side to side, you look alternately from the left wall to the right. Other exercises utilize the memory and imagination to visualize letters on a test card and to increase the contrast between print and the white spaces around it. Techniques such as these are aimed at improving the ability to focus; Bates claimed he was able to cure his own presbyopia by using them.

Although most eye specialists today consider corrective lenses a more effective way of treating refractive disorders, they do find eye exercises—either alone or in combination with glasses—valuable in treating eye problems involving muscle imbalances. (Where Bates differed from this majority view was in believing that refractive disorders, too, are due to a failure of the eye muscles to work properly.) The field of eye muscle and vision training is called *orthoptics*, and it has become an important branch of ophthalmology and optometry. Some eye specialists prescribe and supervise vision training; others work with a specially trained orthoptist.

Retraining the Lazy Eye

Many children's eyes are not tested until they start school. And yet, by then it may be too late to fully correct a rather common and serious vision disorder, called lazy eye or amblyopia. A person with this condition uses only one eye; the other one, although physically healthy and potentially capable of seeing normally, is functionally blind because the brain ignores its messages.

Amblyopia may develop when one eye sees clearly but the other has a vision defect that causes images to be blurred. The brain normally combines the views from the two eyes to produce a three-dimensional picture. But if it is getting conflicting information—a clear, sharp image from one eye and a blurry view from the other—it may learn to ignore the messages from the defective eye. Eventually the unused eye may lose its ability to see, even when the good eye is closed.

Strabismus is an inward or outward turning of one eye. This may result from amblyopia if the eyes are turned in an effort to improve the focus, or if the brain, trying vainly to suppress the blurred image, causes one defective eye to turn so that the image falls on the blind spot in its retina. Strabismus can also cause amblyopia when the external eye muscles do not work together in coordination. Normally the two eyes turn together, moved by the combination of contractions in the sling of six muscles that suspends each eyeball. But if one of the sideward-pulling muscles of one eye is stronger than the corresponding muscle of the other, that eye will be pulled in or out (depending on which muscle is the stronger), producing a cross-eyed or wall-eyed appearance. When the two eyes are not lined up together, the brain cannot combine their images to form a three-dimensional picture. Then the person sees double. Seeing double is a rather uncomfortable sensation, and a young child may learn to suppress the information from one eye. Then the brain gets a clear picture. It lacks the depth of two-eyed vision but makes up for it in sharp detail.

Strabismus can thus be a warning signal that a child may be developing amblyopia. But amblyopia can also occur without strabismus, and a cross-eyed or wall-eyed appearance may sometimes be a false alarm. It is normal for a very young baby's eyes to wander a bit, because eye muscle development is not complete at birth. By about three or four months, the child's eyes should be straight at least most of the time. After that, strabismus is an indication that the child should be checked by an eye specialist.

There are various ways to treat strabismus and amblyopia; often combined approaches are used. The good eye may be covered with a patch, forcing the child to use the weaker eye. Or the doctor may place drops in the good eye to paralyze its focusing. Glasses may be helpful if there are refractive problems; the weaker eye may need a much greater correction than the stronger one. A flashing light or a very bright light may be used to stimulate sight in the amblyopic eye. These measures may be combined with various exercises that teach the eye muscles to work together and train the brain to pay attention to the information from *both* eyes, putting them together into a three-dimensional image. In one type of exercise, the good eye is covered while the weak eye follows a moving object. In another, the eye is trained to fix its gaze on a target (a spot on a card, for example) and then to move it quickly to another. Combinations of prisms, lenses, red-green pictures, mirrors, and other devices may be used in exercises to expand the range over which the eye can focus and converge. After the vision problem has been corrected, some exercises may have to be continued as a routine to keep the visual skills sharp. Sometimes the eyes have to be retrained if the person takes a new job or a hobby that requires different visual skills.

If strabismus does not respond well enough to a combination of glasses and exercises, the eyes can be straightened by surgery. The eye muscles outside the eyeball are adjusted: They are shortened or lengthened or their points of attachment to the eyeball are changed so that their pulls are better balanced. The operation is simple and very safe and produces an immediate improvement of the child's appearance. Eye exercises before and after surgery, though, may be needed to train the eyes to work together.

Recently eye specialists have developed an alternative to surgery for strabismus. A tiny amount of *botulinum toxin* (a bacterial product that causes a deadly form of food poisoning) is injected into the overactive eye muscles. (There is no danger because such a small amount of the poison—a billionth of a gram—is used.) The toxin paralyzes the muscles for a few weeks. During this time the paralyzed muscles become weakened and stretched out, while the opposing muscles work harder and become stronger and tighter, better able to hold the eye in position. By the time the paralyzed muscle recovers, the eyes are properly aligned.

Avoiding Eyestrain

Common sense and some simple precautions can do a great deal to help avoid eyestrain. When you are reading or doing close work, use enough light to feel comfortable. Having the light source directly in front of you or using a single very bright, sharply focused lamp can produce glare that may cause eyestrain and headache. At least two separate light sources—ideally, one above you and one shining from behind, over your shoulder—provide more even, relaxing light for close work. Try to avoid reading when you are very tired or ill, or if you must, break up the reading sessions with frequent rests. Even when you're not tired or ill, stop occasionally to look out at the room or take short breaks to stretch or walk around. This can help to relax the eyes. Reading on a moving vehicle can put a strain on your eyes because the jiggling motion makes it necessary to refocus constantly.

When you watch television, leave at least one lamp on in the room to provide some background light. Sit at least 6 feet from the set and try not to stare fixedly at the screen. The eyes normally shift about constantly, perhaps eighty times a minute. Staring creates an unnatural strain; instead, let your eyes follow the

a board slanted 20° makes reading easier

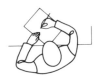

right-handed

left-handed

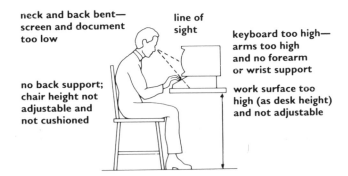

neck and back bent—
screen and document
too low

line of sight

keyboard too high—
arms too high
and no forearm
or wrist support

no back support;
chair height not
adjustable and
not cushioned

work surface too
high (as desk height)
and not adjustable

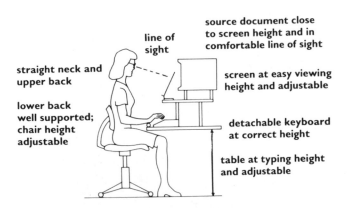

source document close
to screen height and in
comfortable line of sight

line of sight

straight neck and
upper back

screen at easy viewing
height and adjustable

lower back
well supported;
chair height
adjustable

detachable keyboard
at correct height

table at typing height
and adjustable

A well-designed work setup can help avoid eyestrain in activities such as reading, writing, and working with a computer (VDT) terminal.

action on the screen or move about to pick up different details.

The problems of television watching have been magnified for people who work with computers and must gaze at VDTs (*video display terminals*) for hours at a time. Eyestrain, sore eyes, and blurred vision are common complaints among such workers, which is not surprising. Not only must the workers concentrate

Tinted eyeglasses can help to eliminate glare from a VDT terminal.

intensely on the small letters on the screen, but they must constantly shift their focus to the keyboard or to reference materials on the desk beside them.

A sensible arrangement of the work area can help to avoid VDT eyestrain. A comfortable, adjustable chair can help put the terminal user in the best position for comfortable viewing. The center of the VDT screen should be a little below the user's straight-ahead gaze. Reference materials should be as close to the screen as possible, and about the same distance from the eyes as the screen—to avoid frequent switching of focus. Avoiding glare is very important. Windows or lights behind the user may reflect off the screen; so may white clothing. Background lights and desk lamps should be set up or shielded so that they do not shine onto the screen. The VDT screen brightness should be greater than the general room light, and the characters on the screen should be about ten times as bright as the background to provide sharp contrast. Eyeglasses with tints or filters to cut out glare can help to reduce eye fatigue. Frequent rest breaks and alternating VDT work with other kinds of tasks can also help to protect the user's eyes.

The development of civilization has brought new challenges to the eyes that our ancestors did not have to face. Our eyes have proved to be amazingly adaptable, but they do have limits. With each new development, like television and the VDT, new problems arise, and new habits have to be learned to keep the eyes strong and healthy.

FOR FURTHER
READING

Books:

Bates, William H., M.D. *Better Eyesight Without Glasses,* revised ed. New York: Holt, Rinehart & Winston, 1943.

———. *The Bates Method for Better Eyesight Without Glasses.* New York: Holt, Rinehart & Winston, 1981.

Brindze, Ruth. *Look How Many People Wear Glasses: The Magic of Lenses.* New York: Atheneum, 1975.

Esterman, Ben, M.D. *The Eye Book: A Specialist's Guide to Your Eyes and Their Care.* Arlington, VA: Great Ocean Publishers, 1977.

Freese, Arthur S. *The Miracle of Vision.* New York: Harper & Row, 1977.

Gregg, James R., O.D. *The Story of Optometry.* New York: Ronald Press, 1965.

————. *Your Future in New Optometric Careers*. New York: Richards Rosen Press, 1978.

Kelley, Alberta. *Lenses, Spectacles, Eyeglasses, and Contacts: The Story of Vision Aids*. New York: Thomas Nelson, 1978.

Rosanes-Berrett, Marilyn R. *Do You Really Need Eyeglasses?*, revised ed. New York: I.I., Inc., 1983, 1985.

Zinn, Walter J., O.D., and Herbert Solomon, O.D. *The Complete Guide to Eye Care, Eyeglasses, & Contact Lenses*. Hollywood, FL: Frederick Fell, 1977, 1986.

Pamphlets on vision problems, eyeglasses, and contact lenses can be obtained from:

American Academy of Ophthalmology
P.O. Box 7424
San Francisco, CA 94120

American Optometric Association
243 N. Lindbergh Boulevard
St. Louis, MO 63141

Better Vision Institute
230 Park Avenue
New York, NY 10017

INDEX

Page numbers in *italic* type refer to illustrations.

ABOUT
THE
AUTHORS

Dr. Alvin and **Virginia B. Silverstein** have written over seventy books for young readers, mostly in the subject area of biological science. Their success is reflected in both reviews and awards; a number of their books have been cited as Outstanding Science Trade Books for Children by a joint committee of the National Science Teachers Association and the Children's Book Council.

Dr. Alvin Silverstein received his bachelor's degree from Brooklyn College, his master's degree from the University of Pennsylvania, and his doctorate from New York University. He is currently a professor of biology at the College of Staten Island of the City University of New York. Virginia B. Silverstein received her bachelor's degree from the University of Pennsylvania. She works as a translator of Russian scientific literature. They live in rural New Jersey.

MEDORA COMM. SCHOOL LIBRARY

617.7
SIL   Silverstein, Alvin

GLASSES AND CONTACT LENSES: YOUR GUIDE
   TO EYES, EYEWEAR, & EYE CARE

                  33640000027551

617.7
SIL   Silverstein, Alvin

GLASSES AND CONTACT LENSES: YOUR GUIDE
        TO EYES, EYEWEAR, & EYE CARE

MEDORA COMM. SCHOOL LIBRARY

                              ESEA-92